A

in Jerusalem

MY
CUP
RUNNETH
OVER

John C. Bowling

For Marc and Marceil Royer

Whose love for Jerusalem is contagious

CONTENTS

INTRODUCTION

Jerusalem—the name itself evokes a cascade of images. The city stands as a timeless testament to the rich tapestry of human history, faith, and culture. Every corner of the old city seems to tell a story. It is a place that has captured the hearts and minds of people for centuries. With a history spanning nearly four thousand years, Jerusalem is a living museum, where layers of civilizations have left their indelible marks.

In a way, Jerusalem is two cities. There is the Old City, cloistered within ancient walls that date back centuries. The Old City is surrounded by a vibrant modern city filled with restaurants, shops, museums, government offices, and sprawling residential areas. The Old City is divided into four colorfully crowded quarters: the Muslim Quarter, the Christian Quarter, the Jewish Quarter, and the Armenian Quarter. Its ancient walls, cobbled streets, and archaeological sites bear witness to the rise and fall of empires, from the Canaanites and the Israelites to the Romans, Byzantines, Crusaders, Ottomans, and modern-day Israel. Each civilization has made its own contributions to the city's narrative, creating a unique blend of architectural styles, art, and cultural influences.

Jerusalem is a sacred city for Muslims, Jews, and Christians. The Al-Aqsa Mosque and Dome of the Rock stand as iconic symbols of Islamic heritage, while the Western Wall draws Jewish visitors from around the world. Christians find their spiritual epicenter in the *Via Dolorosa*, the garden of Gethsemane, the Church of the Holy Sepulchre, and the Garden Tomb. The daily sounds of the Islamic call to prayer, the Jewish shofar, and a variety of Christian church bells create a symphony of religious diversity.

Beyond its religious significance, Jerusalem is a microcosm of cultural diversity, where various traditions intertwine and coexist. The city's markets, known as *souks*, are bustling hubs of trade where aromas of spices, flavors of Middle Eastern cuisine, and vibrant textiles blend to create an immersive sensory experience. The mixture of spoken languages and the array of traditional garments worn by the inhabitants serve as a reminder of the city's mosaic of cultures.

The gates of Jerusalem form an integral part of the city's collective heritage and identity. They are not merely physical structures but symbolic markers of Jerusalem's historical narrative. The gates of any ancient city were important as a means of providing access to the city while maintaining security. The Bible speaks of the gates of the city of Jerusalem, and many other cities, several times. City gates are where people finalized business deals (see Genesis 23) and arranged marriages (see Ruth 4). Rulers often addressed their subjects from the gates of the city (see 2 Samuel 18).

The walls around Jerusalem—and its gates—have been torn down, built up, and relocated several times. In AD 70, they were destroyed by the Romans, then partially rebuilt, only to be toppled again by an earthquake in 1033. The walls, as they are today, were constructed in the 1500s. To enter the Old

City, one must pass through one of the eight historic gates (more on each individual gate will be said later). Collectively, Jerusalem's gates form an intricate architectural narrative that weaves together the stories of numerous civilizations and religious traditions. Through painstaking excavations and scholarly analysis, these sites have been able to offer students of history, religion, tradition, sociology, anthropology, and archaeology windows into the past, enabling us to comprehend the city's multifaceted history.

A Month in Jerusalem

I have had the privilege of visiting Jerusalem on several occasions as either a member or a leader of a tour. Touring with a professional guide is the best way to gain an overview and initial understanding of the wonders of Israel. However, after a handful of trips, I developed a growing desire not just to visit but to *be* in Jerusalem for a more extended period of time. As a result, I arranged to rent an apartment in Jerusalem for a month with my wife, Jill. Our goal was to walk the streets, talk with those who live there, explore areas not included on tours, and reflect on the wonders of the city of which the psalmist said: "Beautiful in its loftiness, the joy of the whole earth, like the heights of Zaphon is Mount Zion, the city of the Great King. God is in her citadels; he has shown himself to be her fortress" (Psalm 48:2–3). Many cities throughout the world have rich histories, architecture, natural beauty, and enduring appeal—but for me and for many, none of them is like Jerusalem.

A month is not very long, yet it was long enough for us to experience the Holy City in ways generally not available to those passing through on buses and staying in hotels. My appreciation for the people and for the sacred history of Jerusalem was deepened and my personal spiritual journey enriched by this month spent in the city of the Bible.

Israel's airport is named for David Ben-Gurion, who was the first prime minister and the principal founder of the modern State of Israel. He delivered the proclamation of the Israeli Declaration of Independence on May 14, 1948. He is revered in present-day Israel as the father of the nation.

The story of the formal establishment of the State of Israel is one of myriad twists and turns through two world wars and many internal struggles with the Arabic population and the British provincial government. In 1947, a United Nations resolution called for the partition of Palestine into two separate states, one Arabic and one Jewish, with the city of Jerusalem as a separate entity to be governed by a special international counsel. This resolution was immediately rejected by the Arabs. Nonetheless, the Jewish residents of Palestine, with strong international support, seized the moment to declare their independence and establish the State of Israel, with David Ben-Gurion as their leader. Though the tensions and strife that first accompanied the UN patrician plan still exist, Israel celebrated its seventy-fifth anniversary as a nation in May of 2023.

Just three short months after our stay in Israel, the entire nation was turned upside down and inside out. On October 7, 2023, a group known as Hamas launched an attack on Israel from the Gaza Strip, resulting in more than 1,200 deaths and nearly 250 hostages. It was Israel's deadliest day since its independence in 1948. Months of war, destruction, and suffering for innocent civilians followed in the wake of that initial attack.

This ongoing conflict underscores the crying need for peace and reconciliation in our world. It calls to mind the words of Jesus in Matthew 5: "Blessed are the peacemakers, for they will be called children of God" (v. 9).

May the season of Lent inspire a new commitment on the part of Christians worldwide to embrace in fresh ways the message of the gospel, which is centered on a radical form of love that includes loving enemies and forgiving seventy times seven. Only then can hearts be transformed and relationships healed.

When we arrived for our month-long stay in Israel, we decided to spend the first few days in the coastal city of Jaffa. Called Joppa in our biblical stories, it is the place from which Jonah set sail while running from God, and the town of Simon the Tanner, on whose rooftop Peter saw a vision and heard the voice directing him to take the gospel to the gentiles.

After a couple of days in Jaffa and nearby Tel Aviv, we headed to find our apartment in Jerusalem, ideally located in an area known as David's Village. The apartment was modest and well worn, but it had all we needed. Best of all, it was within sight of the Old City.

A Lenten Journey through Jerusalem

The phrase "we cannot contain God's blessings" stayed with me throughout our time in Jerusalem. At nearly every turn, I was confronted with a symbol of God's blessings. We walked the ramparts above the old city, reverently made our way along the *Via Dolorosa*, sat quietly at the Garden Tomb, visited the Upper Room, and prayed among the olive trees in Gethsemane. Each place bore witness to the love of God and particularly to the suffering and sacrifice of Christ.

Drawing on our time in Jerusalem, this book provides an outline for your own journey through the season of Lent using the holy sites of the city as landmarks to chart a course from Jesus's entry into the city, to the upper room, to Gethsemane, to Golgotha, and to the tomb.

Lent is a period of six weeks leading up to Easter that is meant to symbolically replicate the forty days Jesus spent fasting and praying in the wilderness before beginning his public ministry. It is a time for Christians to spiritually prepare ourselves to fully embrace the significance of Easter and its message of hope and redemption. The Lenten season begins with Ash Wednesday and concludes on Holy Saturday. The name "Ash Wednesday" comes from the practice of placing ashes on the foreheads of believers in the shape of a cross as a sign of repentance, humility, and mortality. The ashes are typically made by burning palm fronds from the previous year's Palm Sunday celebrations. The practice of using ashes as a symbol of repentance dates to ancient times, when people used sackcloth and ashes as signs of mourning and penance.

Lent is a time of reflection, repentance, and renewal. It is a time for believers to examine our lives, seek forgiveness, and renew our commitment to our faith. Lent is an opportunity to pause; an invitation to listen; a request to reflect; a summons to prepare; an appeal to repent; a call to commit; a time to reevaluate; a pathway to a deeper life; a plea to come closer to God. Lent encourages us to deepen our relationship with God, examine our lives, and align ourselves with the central themes of the faith, including repentance, forgiveness, and the hope of new life in Christ. It is a season of letting go and letting ourselves break through to a deeper level of commitment in our spiritual lives. In a way, this can only happen as we empty ourselves so we can be made full and whole again. Lent can be a journey that helps us identify those attachments in life that tether us to this world, rather than the next.

How to Use This Study

Take your time through this book. Traditional Lent studies usually reserve Palm Sunday and Holy week for meditating on Jesus's final week in Jerusalem, but this study will spend its entirety in that final week, beginning with the First Sunday in Lent. Lenten considerations are placed alongside personal reflections, geographical-historical information about modern-day Israel, and anecdotes from the author's month in Jerusalem. Spend time with these writings and make your own personal connections to a faith that began in the ancient world and still speaks to all of us today, if we let it.

Read the scriptures. Focus on the events described. Reflect on your own journey. Listen for the Lord to speak.

Each week follows a simple structure.

On **Sunday,** read the abbreviated scripture, short reflection, and prayer.

On **Monday,** read the week's scripture in full and meditate on it.

On **Tuesday, Wednesday,** and **Thursday,** engage with the author's teaching, reflection, and application of the scriptural story.

On **Friday,** ponder a hymn or hymns related to the week's themes.

On **Saturday**, journey with the author through both ancient and modern-day Jerusalem.

A visit to Jerusalem must be more than a sightseeing trip; it should be a pilgrimage that brings one closer to God—and the season of Lent should be the same. It is important not to rush our way toward Easter but to make the intentional, deliberate journey that Jesus made. In so doing, we will not only gain an added appreciation for the Savior but will also be better prepared to celebrate the glories of Easter. To genuinely appreciate the mountaintop, we must first walk through the valley.

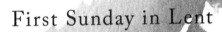

First Sunday in Lent

FACING JERUSALEM: THE CALL TO DISCIPLESHIP

Scripture

Luke 9:18–36, 43–48, 51–62

As the time approached for him to be taken up to heaven, Jesus resolutely set out for Jerusalem.

—Luke 9:51

Reflection

In Luke 9 we find a dramatic turning point in the life of Jesus. Most of his early life has been spent north of Jerusalem, in the region of Galilee, in and around the town of Capernaum. But now the Lord senses that the time has arrived for him to fulfill his mission on earth and do the will of the Father. From this point, he will head south to take his message to the heart of Jerusalem.

Jesus is aware of what will happen when he gets to Jerusalem: he will be confronted by the religious leaders. Within days, the masses that welcomed him heartily into the city will have turned against him. Before the week is up, he will find himself on the cross, being crucified. His decision to go to Jerusalem marks the beginning of the end.

Prayer

Lord, as we begin this Lenten journey, may we hear and heed your call to count the cost. We will need your grace to deny ourselves and take up the cross. Make us willing. Guide our steps and guard our hearts. We pray in the name of the one who "resolutely set out for Jerusalem." Amen.

MONDAY

Read Luke 9:18–36, 43–48, 51–62.

Verses 18–36

Once when Jesus was praying in private and his disciples were with him, he asked them, "Who do the crowds say I am?"

They replied, "Some say John the Baptist; others say Elijah; and still others, that one of the prophets of long ago has come back to life."

"But what about you?" he asked. "Who do you say I am?"

Peter answered, "God's Messiah."

Jesus strictly warned them not to tell this to anyone. And he said, "The Son of Man must suffer many things and be rejected by the elders, the chief priests and the teachers of the law, and he must be killed and on the third day be raised to life."

Then he said to them all: "Whoever wants to be my disciple must deny themselves and take up their cross daily and follow me. For whoever wants to save their life will lose it, but whoever loses their life for me will save it. What good is it for someone to gain the whole world, and yet lose or forfeit their very self? Whoever is ashamed of me and my words, the Son of Man will be ashamed of them when he comes in his glory and in the glory of the Father and of the holy angels. Truly I tell you, some who are standing here will not taste death before they see the kingdom of God."

About eight days after Jesus said this, he took Peter, John and James with him and went up onto a mountain to pray. As he was praying, the appearance of his face changed, and his clothes became as bright as a flash of lightning. Two men, Moses and Elijah, appeared in glorious splendor, talking with Jesus. They spoke about his departure, which he was about to bring to fulfillment at Jerusalem. Peter and his companions were very sleepy, but when they became fully awake, they saw his glory and the two men standing with him. As the men were leaving Jesus, Peter said to him, "Master, it is good for us to be here. Let us put up three shelters—one for you, one for Moses and one for Elijah." (He did not know what he was saying.)

While he was speaking, a cloud appeared and covered them, and they were afraid as they entered the cloud. A voice came from the cloud, saying, "This is my Son, whom I have chosen; listen to him." When the voice had spoken, they found that Jesus was alone. The disciples kept this to themselves and did not tell anyone at that time what they had seen.

Verses 43–48

And they were all amazed at the greatness of God. While everyone was marveling at all that Jesus did, he said to his disciples, "Listen carefully to what I am about to tell you: The Son of Man is going to be delivered into the hands of men." But they did not understand what this meant. It was hidden from them, so that they did not grasp it, and they were afraid to ask him about it. An argument started among the disciples as to which of them would be the greatest. Jesus, knowing their thoughts, took a little child and had him stand beside him. Then he said to them, "Whoever welcomes this little child in my name welcomes me; and whoever welcomes me welcomes the one who sent me. For it is the one who is least among you all who is the greatest."

Verses 51–62

As the time approached for him to be taken up to heaven, Jesus resolutely set out for Jerusalem. And he sent messengers on ahead, who went into a Samaritan village to get things ready for him; but the people there did not welcome him, because he was heading for Jerusalem. When the disciples James and John saw this, they asked, "Lord, do you want us to call fire down from heaven to destroy them?" But Jesus turned and rebuked them. Then he and his disciples went to another village. As they were walking along the road, a man said to him, "I will follow you wherever you go."

Jesus replied, "Foxes have dens and birds have nests, but the Son of Man has no place to lay his head."

He said to another man, "Follow me."

But he replied, "Lord, first let me go and bury my father."

Jesus said to him, "Let the dead bury their own dead, but you go and proclaim the kingdom of God."

Still another said, "I will follow you, Lord; but first let me go back and say goodbye to my family."

Jesus replied, "No one who puts a hand to the plow and looks back is fit for service in the kingdom of God."

TUESDAY

Reflection

Throughout Luke 9, Jesus gives his attention to two primary concerns. First, he is preparing himself to head toward Jerusalem and the cross. Second, he wishes to prepare his followers for what is about to take place.

He begins by asking, "Who have the crowds been saying I am?"

After their replies, he asks the more salient question: "Who do *you* say I am?"

To which Peter responds, "You are the Christ we have been waiting for—the very Son of God."

Now assured that the disciples recognize him, Jesus follows with a curious admonition and a sober prediction. He strictly warns and commands them to keep their knowledge of his identity to themselves, saying, "The Son of Man must suffer many things and be rejected by the elders, the chief priests and the teachers of the law, and he must be killed and on the third day be raised to life" (Luke 9:22). Then the Lord turns his attention to the call to discipleship, saying, "Whoever wants to be my disciple must deny themselves and take up their cross daily and follow me. For whoever wants to save their life will lose it, but whoever loses their life for me will save it" (vv. 23–24).

It seems that, up to this time, the Twelve have been followers of Jesus, but perhaps they have not yet become fully dedicated disciples. Thus, Jesus confronts them with the cost of discipleship—deny yourself, take up your cross, and then—follow me. Jesus is calling them to make a deeper commitment.

For Additional Meditation

Colossians 3:1–17
Matthew 10:16–42

These scriptures explore what a deeper commitment to Jesus might look like. Consider how closely aligned your life today is with the kind of life these scriptures describe.

_____

_____

_____

_____

_____

_____

_____

_____

WEDNESDAY

Reflection

After Jesus calls his disciples to a deeper commitment, he withdraws to continue preparing himself for what he knows is about to happen. He takes Peter, James, and John up a mountain to pray. There, he is transfigured and joined by Moses and Elijah (representing the Law and the Prophets), who appear in glory and speak of what he is about to accomplish in Jerusalem. All of this fanfare is accompanied by the voice of the Father declaring, "This is my Son, whom I have chosen; listen to him" (Luke 9:35).

Following the transfiguration, we see Jesus's resolve—his sheer determination—to obey God's will regardless of the cost. He intently sets his face to go to Jerusalem. From a human standpoint, he has nothing to gain and everything to lose. Yet Jesus will not be dissuaded. He understands that this was the will of the Father and also his destiny.

He knows exactly what he is doing and why he is doing it. This knowledge is implicit in the language of the text. Luke does not say that Jesus charts his path toward Jerusalem because he has run out of things to do in Capernaum, or because the Galileans will not listen to what he has to say, or because he thinks he might have better opportunities in Jerusalem. No, instead Luke declares that "the time [was approaching] for him to be taken up to heaven" and that, therefore, "Jesus resolutely set out for Jerusalem" (9:51). When we do something "resolutely," we aren't doing it because it is convenient or fun. The same is true for Jesus. He sets out resolutely in obedience to the plan of the Father. Paul tells us that God was in Christ, reconciling the world to himself (see 2 Corinthians 5:19). Once Jesus has determined to follow this course, he will allow nothing to stand in his way.

Some time ago, I read of a sermon that used a recurring phrase to describe the Lord's commitment to the will of the Father. The phrase was, *He kept on walking.* That certainly describes Jesus as he turns his face toward Jerusalem. Even though the adoring crowds that greet him on Palm Sunday will turn against him in just a few days, he keeps on walking. When he is confronted with betrayal by one of the Twelve, he keeps on walking. Even in the face of scourging and execution, he keeps on walking.

This is the essence of a life of faith—to keep on walking, seeking God's will above all else. What a contrast this is to the present culture in which we live. The world tells us to play it safe; weigh the pros and cons; keep our options open; do what makes *you* happy; stick to your plan! Jesus, on the other hand, teaches his disciples: "Seek first his kingdom and his righteousness, and all these things will be given to you as well" (Matthew 6:33).

For Additional Meditation

John 15:18–27
Acts 6:8–15

Read these scriptures and ponder how they demonstrate an attitude consistent with the way Jesus *kept on walking*.

THURSDAY

Reflection

Lent calls us to set our set our sights on Christ and his kingdom, forsaking all else for the sake of the gospel. We must be willing to take up the cross. To illustrate the commitment the Lord seeks, Luke records three encounters that take place as Jesus and the Twelve head toward Jerusalem.

The **first would-be disciple** came to Jesus saying, "I will follow you wherever you go" (Luke 9:57). In response, Jesus told him, "Foxes have dens and birds have nests, but the Son of Man has no place to lay his head" (v. 58). The Lord seeks to let this individual know something of the cost involved. Following Jesus is not a walk on the red carpet or a flower-strewn pathway. Jesus is really asking, "Do you still want to follow me, even if it means forsaking your worldly comfort and earthly sense of security?"

There is a cost to following Jesus. Today, we too often magnify the blessings of being a Christ follower while minimizing the cost. The Lenten season is a megaphone through which we hear the word of the Lord reminding us of the commitment needed to follow Jesus.

On another occasion, Jesus told his disciples,

> I am sending you out like sheep among wolves. Therefore be as shrewd as snakes and as innocent as doves. Be on

your guard; you will be handed over to the local councils and be flogged in the synagogues. On my account you will be brought before governors and kings as witnesses to them and to the Gentiles. . . . Brother will betray brother to death, and a father his child; children will rebel against their parents and have them put to death. You will be hated by everyone because of me, but the one who stands firm to the end will be saved.
(Matthew 10:16–18, 21–22)

Christian discipleship is not for the faint of heart.

Neither is it for those with a dual allegiance, as seen in the second encounter. **Would-be disciple number two** enters the scene and, at first, does not say a word to Jesus. Instead, Jesus calls to him, saying, "Follow me" (Luke 9:59). When Jesus said that to his first disciples, they dropped their nets and came running. However, this individual hesitates, saying, "Lord, first let me go and bury my father" (v. 59). In response, Jesus replied, "Let the dead bury their own dead, but you go and proclaim the kingdom of God" (v. 60).

That sounds harsh at first. However, Jesus is not addressing the planning of a funeral service but divided loyalties. It is possible that the man's father was not actually dead or dying but simply growing older. Thus, the request was in essence, *Let me fulfill my obligation to my father for the next few years. Then, after he's gone, when it is more convenient for me, I'll be free to follow you.*

Devotion to others is important, but it must come second to our commitment to following Jesus. In the language of the

Old Testament, "You shall have no other gods before me" (Exodus 20:3).

Later in the Gospel of Luke we find these words of Jesus: "If anyone comes to me and does not hate father and mother, wife and children, brothers and sisters—yes, even their own life— such a person cannot be my disciple" (14:26). Viewing this verse in a positive light, it is saying, *Put God first and let others find their rightful place in your life.*

The third would-be follower said, "I will follow you, Lord; but first let me go back and say goodbye to my family" (9:61). But Jesus said to him, "No one who puts a hand to the plow and looks back is fit for service in the kingdom of God" (v. 62).

The message here is clear: Don't look back. To look back is to invite regrets, foster nostalgia, and live in retrospect. There is a reason the windshield of an automobile is so much larger than the rearview mirror. Even though one needs to look back occasionally, it is more important to have a wide, clear view facing forward to safely navigate the twists and turns of the road.

Looking back leads us to second-guess and wonder, *Did I make the right decision? What if I'd done this? What if I hadn't done that?* To look back is to hold on to a memory rather than claim a promise. It is to deny the possibility that what will be is just as important as, if not more important than, what has been.

I grew up in a small farming community in western Ohio. However, we did not live *on* a farm. We lived in town, where my father ran the newspaper. Therefore, even though I am from a rural area, I've never plowed a field. Nonetheless, it is my understanding that the only way to plow a straight furrow is to pick a point in the distance and proceed directly toward it, keeping your eyes fixed on that spot. If you look to the left, you'll veer to the left. If you look to the right, you'll veer to the right. If you select a point in front of you and keep your eyes focused on it, you will plow a straight line every time. Just so, as we follow Jesus, we are to fix our eyes on him.

In the book of Hebrews, we find this admonition:

> Therefore, since we are surrounded by such a great cloud of witnesses, let us throw off everything that hinders and the sin that so easily entangles. And let us run with perseverance the race marked out for us, fixing our eyes on Jesus, the pioneer and perfecter of faith. For the joy set before him he endured the cross, scorning its shame, and sat down at the right hand of the throne of God. Consider him who endured such opposition from sinners, so that you will not grow weary and lose heart (Hebrews 12:1–3)

Similarly, Paul put it this way: "Brothers and sisters, I do not consider myself yet to have taken hold of it. But one thing I do: Forgetting what is behind and straining toward what is ahead, I press on toward the goal to win the prize for which God has called me heavenward in Christ Jesus" (Philippians 3:13–14).

When Jesus resolved to go to Jerusalem, he determined not to allow anything to stand in his way. In doing so, he laid down his life for the sins of the world, that we might be reconciled to God. In response, we are to set our sights on him and seek first his kingdom above all else.

For Additional Meditation

James 1:2–18
1 Peter 4:12–19

Read these scriptures and consider how they speak to the idea of keeping our eyes on Jesus and on the goal ahead of us.

_____

_____

_____

_____

_____

_____

_____

_____

_____

_____

_____

_____

_____

_____

_____

_____

_____

_____

_____

_____

_____

_____

_____

_____

_____

FRIDAY

Ponder the words of these old familiar hymns as you continue to think on what you've studied and learned this week.

Turn Your Eyes upon Jesus (#327, refrain)

Turn your eyes upon Jesus
Look full in his wonderful face
And the things of earth will grow strangely dim
In the light of his glory and grace

I Have Decided to Follow Jesus (#468)

I have decided to follow Jesus
I have decided to follow Jesus
I have decided to follow Jesus
No turning back, no turning back

The world behind me, the cross before me
The world behind me, the cross before me
The world behind me, the cross before me
No turning back, no turning back.

Though none go with me, still I will follow
Though none go with me, still I will follow
Though none go with me, still I will follow
No turning back, no turning back.

Jesus, I My Cross Have Taken (#471)

Jesus, I my cross have taken
All to leave and follow thee
Destitute, despised, forsaken
Thou from hence my all shall be

Perish every fond ambition
All I've sought, and hoped and known
Yet how rich is my condition
God and heaven are still my own!

SATURDAY IN JERUSALEM

Because our residence was so close, we used the Jaffa Gate regularly during our month-long stay in Jerusalem. It was our primary entrance into the Old City, giving us the opportunity to become familiar and get acquainted with the various businesses and a few of the vendors whose stalls lined the narrow passageway. Little by little, we began to feel less like visitors.

The Jaffa Gate

The Jaffa Gate, located at the center of the western edge of the Old City, near the site of Herod's palace, is perhaps one of the most heavily traveled entrances into the Old City. It was constructed in 1538, during the Ottoman occupation. The Ottomans defeated the Mamelukes in 1517 and took over the city. In 1520, Sultan Suleiman the Magnificent decided to use the city as a base for his rule over the area. This decision led to the rebuilding of the walls in 1536–41. Those walls still stand today. Their circumference is about two and a half miles. These walls separate the Old City from the sprawling modern city that is scattered across the surrounding hills. As we passed through the Jaffa Gate, we entered a previous time—hundreds and even thousands of years earlier.

The German Kaiser Wilhelm II visited Jerusalem in 1898. He was dead set on riding his horse into the city, but a local prophecy foretold that Jerusalem would be seized by a ruler on a white horse entering through the Jaffa Gate. Rather than allow such an incendiary scene, the authorities made a breach in the wall just by the official gate, through which the Kaiser might enter.

During World War I, the Battle of Jerusalem in December 1917 resulted in the city falling to British forces led by General Edmund Allenby. This victory was the end of the nearly four-hundred-year Ottoman rule over Jerusalem. A few days after the British gained control, General Allenby arranged for his official entrance into the city—a carefully choreographed occasion, rich in imagery and designed with surprising nuance and sensitivity. Rather than enter on horseback, General Allenby dismounted at the Jaffa Gate and walked into the Old City. Allenby was aware of the great symbolism associated with his entrance into the city. Daniel 12:12 predicts blessings for Jerusalem after 1,335 days. Interestingly, the year 1917 in the Islamic calendar was the year 1335. Allenby also recalled Jesus entering the Holy City riding on a donkey. He did not wish to replicate this action or style himself as a modern Messiah. Thus, he conducted himself with conspicuous humility by dismounting and walking through the Jaffa Gate. He understood the symbolism. He had come not as a conqueror nor as a savior but as a liberator.

Herod's Gate

Known in Arabic as *Bab al-Zahra*—"Flower Gate"—Herod's Gate is another of the main entrances to Jerusalem's Old City. It is in the northeastern part of the city, adjacent to the Muslim Quarter. The gate derives its name from Herod the Great, the Roman-appointed king of Judea in the first century BC. Although Herod's Gate was not directly commissioned *by* the king for whom it is named, the name pays homage to his influential reign. Herod was known for his ambitious building projects throughout the region, including the expansion and beautification of Jerusalem. While he is most renowned for the construction of the second temple, his impact on the city's architecture extends beyond religious structures.

The naming of Herod's Gate underscores his broader influence on the urban landscape of Jerusalem. The gate itself features an imposing stone facade, adorned with intricate details and decorative elements. It consists of a central arch flanked by two smaller arches that were once used for pedestrian access. The overall design reflects a harmonious blend of Roman, Byzantine, and Islamic architectural influences.

The Eastern Gate

The Eastern Gate, also known as the Golden Gate or the Gate of Mercy, holds immense historic and religious significance in the Old City. Although the gate's exact origins are disputed, most scholars trace it back to the time of the second Jewish temple in the sixth century BC. Located on the eastern wall, it has witnessed numerous events throughout the centuries, making it a revered and iconic structure. The gate has undergone several reconstructions due to damage from various conflicts, including the Roman destruction of Jerusalem in

70 AD and the subsequent Byzantine, Arab, and Crusader occupations.

In addition to its historical legacy, the Eastern Gate holds religious significance for Judaism, Christianity, and Islam. In Judaism, it is believed to be the gate through which the Messiah will enter Jerusalem during the messianic era. Thus, according to Jewish tradition, the gate was sealed by the Ottoman sultan Suleiman the Magnificent in the sixteenth century to prevent the Messiah's entry and to discourage Jewish aspirations for rebuilding the temple.

For Christians, the Eastern Gate is associated with Jesus's triumphant entry into Jerusalem. This is perhaps the gate through which Jesus entered Jerusalem during the events leading up to his crucifixion. As a result, the gate serves as a pilgrimage site for Christians who seek to retrace the footsteps of Jesus.

The gate's architecture reflects the diverse cultural influences that have shaped Jerusalem throughout history. From its Byzantine-style pillars to Islamic-style domes, the gate embodies the city's multicultural heritage and serves as a testament to the coexistence of different traditions.

The Eastern Gate also represents the resilience and endurance of the people of Jerusalem. Despite the gate's historical conflicts and various periods of closure, it has remained a symbol of hope, peace, and faith. Its rich history, religious significance, and cultural symbolism make it an integral part of Jerusalem's heritage.

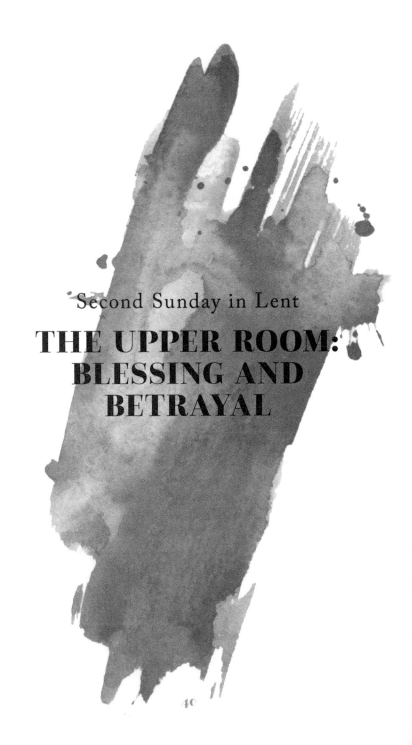

Second Sunday in Lent

THE UPPER ROOM: BLESSING AND BETRAYAL

Scripture

Luke 22:1–34; John 13:1–17

Now that you know these things, you will be blessed if you do them.
—John 13:17

The Son of Man will go as it has been decreed. But woe to that man who betrays him!
—Luke 22:22

Reflection

We now turn our attention to the themes of blessing and betrayal, with an emphasis on the events of the Passover meal Jesus shared with his disciples right before his arrest and crucifixion. Among the numerous sacred sites in the Old City, the Upper Room stands out as a place of distinct significance.

The present-day Upper Room that pilgrims and tourists visit is on the second story of a building built by the Crusaders in the twelfth century as part of the Church of St. Mary of Zion. The Gothic columns seen there today are from that era. The buildings around the Upper Room are the remains of a Franciscan medieval friary from around 1335. The Upper Room was transformed into a mosque by the Ottomans in 1524; thus, a prayer niche is embedded on the south wall, directed toward the Islamic cities of Mecca and Medina.

Although the present structure does not date to the time of Christ, archaeological and historical data strongly suggest that this was the physical site of the room used by Jesus as he gathered with his disciples for their Passover meal. The Upper Room has also been identified as the location of the first Jewish-Christian church. Evidence of this can be found in the massive stones in the Torah Ark Niche of the church on the first floor.

The Upper Room was a pivotal place for Jesus and his disciples. According to the Gospels of Matthew, Mark, and Luke, Jesus sent two of his disciples ahead of him to prepare for the Passover feast. They were guided to the Upper Room, where they made the necessary arrangements for the meal. This event, commonly called the Last Supper, links Passover with the sacrificial nature of Jesus's impending crucifixion. This meal was a profound moment of revelation and communion with his closest followers.

Prayer

(Based on Psalm 139)

Lord, you know me because you have searched me. You know me because you knit me in my mother's womb. You know my actions, my motivations, my thoughts. There is nowhere I could go on this entire earth and not find you there. Reveal to me your will and your path, that I might follow you. Lead me and guide me, that the glory may be yours. Amen.

MONDAY

Read Luke 22:1–34.

Now the Festival of Unleavened Bread, called the Passover, was approaching, and the chief priests and the teachers of the law were looking for some way to get rid of Jesus, for they were afraid of the people. Then Satan entered Judas, called Iscariot, one of the Twelve. And Judas went to the chief priests and the officers of the temple guard and discussed with them how he might betray Jesus. They were delighted and agreed to give him money. He consented, and watched for an opportunity to hand Jesus over to them when no crowd was present. Then came the day of Unleavened Bread on which the Passover lamb had to be sacrificed. Jesus sent Peter and John, saying, "Go and make preparations for us to eat the Passover."

"Where do you want us to prepare for it?" they asked.

He replied, "As you enter the city, a man carrying a jar of water will meet you. Follow him to the house that he enters, and say to the owner of the house, 'The Teacher asks: Where is the guest room, where I may eat the Passover with my disciples?' He will show you a large room upstairs, all furnished. Make preparations there." They left and found things just as Jesus had told them. So they prepared the Passover.

When the hour came, Jesus and his apostles reclined at the table. And he said to them, "I have eagerly desired to eat this Passover with you before I suffer. For I tell you, I will not eat it again until it finds fulfillment in the kingdom of God." After taking the cup, he gave thanks and said, "Take this and divide it among you. For I tell you I will not drink again from the fruit of the vine until the kingdom of God comes." And he took bread, gave thanks and broke it, and gave it to them, saying, "This is my body given for you; do this in remembrance of me." In the same way, after the supper he took the cup, saying, "This cup is the new covenant in my blood, which is poured out for you. But the hand of him who is going to betray me is with mine on the table. The Son of Man will go as it has been decreed. But woe to that man who betrays him!" They began to question among themselves which of them it might be who would do this.

A dispute also arose among them as to which of them was considered to be greatest. Jesus said to them, "The kings of the Gentiles lord it over them; and those who exercise authority over them call themselves Benefactors. But you are not to be like that. Instead, the greatest among you should be like the youngest, and the one who rules like the one who serves. For who is greater, the one who is at the table or the one who serves? Is it not the one who is at the table? But I am among you as one who serves. You are those who have stood by me in my trials. And I confer on you a kingdom, just as my Father conferred one on me, so that you may eat and drink at my table in my kingdom and sit on thrones, judging the twelve tribes of Israel. Simon, Simon, Satan has asked to sift all of you as wheat. But I have prayed for you, Simon, that your faith may not fail. And when you have turned back, strengthen your brothers."

But he replied, "Lord, I am ready to go with you to prison and to death."

Jesus answered, "I tell you, Peter, before the rooster crows today, you will deny three times that you know me."

TUESDAY

Read John 13:1–17.

It was just before the Passover Festival. Jesus knew that the hour had come for him to leave this world and go to the Father. Having loved his own who were in the world, he loved them to the end. The evening meal was in progress, and the devil had already prompted Judas, the son of Simon Iscariot, to betray Jesus. Jesus knew that the Father had put all things under his power, and that he had come from God and was returning to God; so he got up from the meal, took off his outer clothing, and wrapped a towel around his waist. After that, he poured water into a basin and began to wash his disciples' feet, drying them with the towel that was wrapped around him.

He came to Simon Peter, who said to him, "Lord, are you going to wash my feet?"

Jesus replied, "You do not realize now what I am doing, but later you will understand."

"No," said Peter, "you shall never wash my feet."

Jesus answered, "Unless I wash you, you have no part with me."

"Then, Lord," Simon Peter replied, "not just my feet but my hands and my head as well!"

Jesus answered, "Those who have had a bath need only to wash their feet; their whole body is clean. And you are clean, though not every one of you." For he knew who was going to betray him, and that was why he said not every one was clean.

When he had finished washing their feet, he put on his clothes and returned to his place. "Do you understand what I have done for you?" he asked them. "You call me 'Teacher' and 'Lord,' and rightly so, for that is what I am. Now that I, your Lord and Teacher, have washed your feet, you also should wash one another's feet. I have set you an example that you should do as I have done for you. Very truly I tell you, no servant is greater than his master, nor is a messenger greater than the one who sent him. Now that you know these things, you will be blessed if you do them.

WEDNESDAY

Reflection

As the scriptures tell us, the Upper Room is where Jesus shared a final meal with his disciples before his crucifixion. During this meal, Jesus washed the feet of the disciples and broke the news to them that one of them was going to betray him. As Jesus reclined at the table with his disciples, he knew the hour of his crucifixion was drawing near. Yet, even as he bore the weight of his impending suffering, Jesus displayed great humility and love by washing the feet of his disciples. This act serves as a poignant reminder that true greatness is found in serving others.

Perhaps the most significant moment during the meal was when Jesus instituted the sacrament of holy Communion. He took bread, blessed it, and broke it, saying, "This is my body given for you; do this in remembrance of me" (Luke 22:19). In these words, Jesus foreshadowed his sacrificial death on the cross. This enduring sacrament invites us, whenever we partake of it today, to remember and share symbolically in his sacrifice. We are reminded of Christ's body broken for us—his sacrifice that brings us forgiveness and salvation.

In a similar manner, Jesus took the cup and declared, "This cup is the new covenant in my blood, which is poured out for you" (v. 20). Through his shed blood, Jesus established a new covenant between God and humanity. The blood of Jesus signifies the forgiveness of sins and the restoration of our relationship with God. When we partake of the cup, we are to remember the blood of Christ that cleanses us from all unrighteousness and grants us eternal life.

Jesus also emphasized the importance of unity among his followers during this Passover meal. The account of this supper in John records him praying for his disciples, saying, "Holy Father, protect them by the power of your name . . . so that they may be one as we are one" (17:11). This prayer highlights the significance of unity within the body of Christ, which is also embedded in the universal nature of the sacrament of Communion.

For Additional Meditation

John 13:18–38
John 14:1–31
John 15:1–17

Chapters 13 through 17 in the Gospel of John record what is known as the Upper Room Discourse. These chapters comprise the primary readings for the second week in Lent. Today and tomorrow, meditate on these chapters, keeping in mind their context of the upper room and the Passover meal and what Jesus knew lay ahead for him.

THURSDAY

Reflection

The drama of the Last Supper unfolds in four scenes: the preparation, the foot washing, the blessing of the bread and cup, followed by the Lord's prediction of betrayal. Each scene reveals a point of application for us today.

The Preparation

It was the first day of the Feast of Unleavened Bread, an eight-day feast that began with the observance of the Passover. There was much preparation to be done. The disciples inquired of Jesus where they would observe the feast so they could begin those very preparations. Jesus tells them there is a certain man in the city to whom they are to go, informing him that Jesus needs a space to celebrate the feast. This man, according to the Gospels, would be identified as the one who is carrying a water pitcher.

The disciples would have to obtain unleavened bread, spices, fruit, and a lamb. There was a lot of preparation that went into the observance of Passover. The borrowed room had to be searched for any trace of yeast. Any crumb of regular—or leavened—bread had to be removed. Yeast represented the evil influence of Egypt that the Jews left behind at the exodus. Yeast came to be known as the influence of sin.

Just as the disciples had to prepare for the meal, so must we prepare for taking the Lord's Supper. We are to observe the sacrament, according to Paul, with prepared hearts. Paul said we are not to observe in an unworthy manner: "So then, whoever eats the bread or drinks the cup of the Lord in an unworthy manner will be guilty of sinning against the body and blood of the Lord. Everyone ought to examine themselves before they eat of the bread and drink from the cup. For those who eat and drink without discerning the body of Christ eat and drink judgment on themselves" (1 Corinthians 11:27–29). Of course, this scripture does not mean we should skip Communion if we made a mistake recently or even if we have intentionally sinned in the last few days. It means we should examine ourselves first and then approach the Lord's Table with the right attitude and proper heart.

The Foot Washing

Walking in sandals on the roads of the first century made it imperative for feet to be washed before a communal meal. People ate reclining at low tables, and feet were very much nearby. For Jesus, the washing of the disciples' feet was a display of his humility and servanthood. He was doing the task that was generally assigned to the lowliest servants. For the disciples, this washing of their feet displayed a mindset that directly contrasted with their own thinking and behavior.

The disciples must have been stunned at this act of humility—Jesus, their Lord and Master, washing the feet of his disciples. Foot washing should more properly have been *their* work, but no one volunteered. This moment underscored that Jesus came to earth not as king and conqueror but as the suffering servant of Isaiah 53. As noted in Matthew 20:28: "just as the Son of Man did not come to be served, but to serve, and to give his life as a ransom for many."

The humility expressed by Jesus's act with towel and basin foreshadowed his ultimate act of humility and love on the cross, and it also set the disciples' lack of humility in stark contrast. Indeed, they had recently been arguing among themselves as to which of them was the greatest. Evidently, there was no servant present in the upper room to wash their feet, and it never occurred to them to wash one another's feet. When the Lord himself stooped to this lowly task, they were stunned.

When Jesus finished, he told them (and us), "I have set you an example that you should do as I have done for you" (John 13:15). As his followers, we are to emulate him, serving one another in lowliness of heart and mind, seeking to build one another up in humility and love. Foot washing takes on different forms these days. It may mean caring for the sick, visiting the lonely, or cutting the grass for someone who has mobility issues. When we seek preeminence, neglect to serve others, or refuse to forgive, we displease the Lord. True greatness in his kingdom is attained by those with servant hearts, and they will be greatly blessed.

The Bread and the Cup

Again Jesus interrupted the Passover meal, this time in order to transform it into the Lord's Supper. He took the bread and told his disciples that it now represented his body. He took the cup of wine and said it now represented his blood, shed for many for the remission of sins. Remission means "release," as in the cancellation of a debt. The shedding of Jesus's blood on the cross was so that people might experience release from the penalty of sin. His broken body and shed blood provided salvation.

The disciples were to receive the bread, which represented the body of Christ, and drink the wine, which represented his blood. I think of the statement by my friend Dr. David, when we visited his home for a Saturday Shabbat meal. You are never to ask for bread, he said. We are not beggars. We receive the bread as children of our heavenly Father.

This represents the wonderful truth that we may have life and forgiveness and release from the power of sin by receiving, by faith, Christ's broken body and blood on our behalf. This is the new covenant, which we are to remember and celebrate each time we participate in the sacrament of holy Communion. This sacrament is also known as the Eucharist, from the Greek *eucharistia* for "thanksgiving."

The Prediction of Betrayal

Jesus next interjected a startling prediction into the traditional Passover meal. He said, "One of you will betray me." The disciples had already been told by Jesus that he would be delivered into the hands of the enemy, but they were *not* told until this moment that one of their own number would betray him. This news cut the disciples to the heart, and each man began to question himself. The Greek words indicate that they were deeply sorrowful and violently shaken.

Each disciple, looking around the table, asked the same question: "Who is it?" There's doubt; there's concern; there's questioning of their own hearts. *Surely it isn't me, is it?*

Each conducted a spiritual inventory and wondered who among them would betray Jesus. In Luke's account, Peter was the only who spoke. He declared boldly that he was ready to go with Jesus to prison and even to death. These words would later come back to haunt him.

Judas, of course, knew he was the one. In one way, the last person the disciples would have suspected was Judas. He was the treasurer—the one who was, perhaps, trusted the most. At this point, Judas left the table and went forth to summon the guards to Gethsemane.

Just as the disciples had to examine their hearts, the Lenten season provides an extended time for us to do the same.

For Additional Meditation

John 15:18–27
John 16:1–33
John 17:1–26

Continue meditating on the Upper Room Discourse chapters from John, keeping in mind their context and what Jesus knew lay ahead for him.

_____

_____

_____

_____

_____

_____

_____

_____

_____

_____

_____

FRIDAY

Ponder the words of these old familiar hymns as you continue to think on what you've studied and learned this week.

Here at Thy Table, Lord (#745)

Here at thy table, Lord, this sacred hour
O let us feel thee near in loving power
Calling our thoughts away from self and sin
As to thy banquet hall we enter in

Come then, O holy Christ; feed us, we pray
Touch with thy pierced hand each common day
Making this earthly life full of thy grace
Till in the home of heaven we find our place

Let Us Break Bread Together (#748)

Let us break bread together on our knees
Let us break bread together on our knees
When I fall on my knees with my face to the rising sun
O Lord, have mercy on me

Let us drink the cup together on our knees
Let us drink the cup together on our knees
When I fall on my knees with my face to the rising sun
O Lord, have mercy on me

Now Let Us from This Table Rise (#751)

Now let us from this table rise
Renewed in body, mind and soul
With Christ we die and live again
His selfless love has made us whole

To fill each human house with love
It is the sacrament of care
The work that Christ began to do
We humbly pledge ourselves to share

SATURDAY IN JERUSALEM

Zion Gate

Zion Gate is near the west corner of the southern wall that connects King David's tomb and the Upper Room to the Jewish Quarter of the Old City. It holds a prominent place as a gateway to Jerusalem's rich history and religious significance. Zion Gate, known also as *Sha'ar Tzion* in Hebrew, has seen the rise and fall of empires, the struggles of different civilizations, and the movements of countless pilgrims and tourists.

During the 1948 Arab-Israeli War, Zion Gate found itself at the heart of intense fighting. The Jordanian forces, who controlled the Old City during that time, targeted the gate to cut off the Jewish Quarter from the rest of Jerusalem. The defenders valiantly held their ground, but when the battle eventually ended, the Jewish Quarter lay in ruins, including many structures surrounding Zion Gate. The restored Zion Gate serves as a symbol of resilience and determination for the Jewish people. It stands as a testament to their enduring connection to the land and their commitment to preserving their heritage.

Zion Gate's architecture is a blend of Ottoman and Crusader influences, reflecting the various periods of Jerusalem's history. Its solid stone structure, narrow entrance, and characteristic pointed arches evoke a sense of strength and grandeur. Above the gate, one can find engraved stone inscriptions in both Arabic and Hebrew, further emphasizing the gate's historical and multicultural significance.

Passing through Zion Gate, one enters the Jewish Quarter, a vibrant area brimming with life, history, and religious devotion. Within the narrow streets of the Jewish Quarter, visitors can explore ancient synagogues, archaeological sites, and bustling markets. The area is also home to numerous educational institutions, ensuring the preservation of Jewish scholarship and intellectual pursuits.

The Lions' Gate

The Lions' Gate stands as a majestic entryway, underscoring the rich history and cultural importance of this ancient city. It is situated on the eastern wall of the Old City of Jerusalem, adjacent to the Temple Mount, facing the Mount of Olives. Constructed during the Ottoman period in the 16th century, the gate gained its name from the pair of lion sculptures flanking its entrance.

For Christians, the Lion's Gate holds special meaning, for it is also known as Saint Stephen's Gate. It is generally understood that Stephen, the first Christian martyr, was killed in the Kidron Valley, just below the gate. After being arrested, Stephen was brought before the Sanhedrin for questioning. In response, he boldly proclaimed the story of Jesus and accused them, saying: "You stiff-necked people! Your hearts and ears are still uncircumcised. You are just like your ancestors: You always resist the Holy Spirit! Was there ever a prophet your

ancestors did not persecute? They even killed those who predicted the coming of the Righteous One. And now you have
betrayed and murdered him—you who have received the law
that was given through angels but have not obeyed it" (Acts
7:51–53). At that point, the Sanhedrin became furious and
dragged Stephen outside the city walls and began to stone
him. While they were stoning him, Stephen prayed that the
Lord would receive his spirit and that God would forgive those
stoning him.

The Lions' Gate is also significant to the Jews. Its proximity to
the Western Wall, or the Wailing Wall—the holiest site in Judaism—makes it a vital access point for Jewish worshipers. The
Lions' Gate is also associated with several significant events in
Jewish history. It is believed to be the probable location of the
biblical Sheep Gate, through which the sheep used for sacrificial offerings were brought into the temple.

The New Gate

The New Gate is located on the northwestern side of the city
walls, facing the modern city and adjacent to the Christian
Quarter. The New Gate was constructed in the late nineteenth
century in response to the Christian community's petition to
the governing officials for a gate that led directly into their
quarter.

Over the years, the New Gate has witnessed its share of
historical events and conflicts, including the British Mandate
period, the Arab-Israeli conflicts, and the Six-Day War in

1967. The gate has undergone renovations and modifications to accommodate modern needs while preserving its historical character.

The significance of the New Gate lies in its strategic location and its role in connecting the Old City with the modern city of Jerusalem. The gate serves as a major entry point for Christian tourists, pilgrims, and residents because it provides direct access to important Christian sites like the Church of the Holy Sepulchre and others.

The Dung Gate

The Dung Gate is another of the historic gates leading into the Old City of Jerusalem. It holds both historical and religious significance and has played a crucial role in the city's history. It is located on the southern wall of the city, facing the Kidron Valley. The current gate dates back to the sixteenth century, but its history can be traced to earlier periods.

The Dung Gate is mentioned in the Hebrew Bible, specifically in Nehemiah. During the restoration of Jerusalem's walls in the fifth century BC, the Dung Gate was one of the gates repaired by the Israelites under Nehemiah's leadership. According to Jewish tradition, it is believed that the sacrificial ashes from the temple were taken out through this gate and disposed of in the Kidron Valley. Therefore, the gate was associated with ritual purity and cleanliness.

Excavations near the Dung Gate have yielded significant archaeological discoveries. One of the most notable finds was the

Jerusalem City Wall Ostracon, a clay tablet with an ancient Hebrew inscription dating back to the eighth century BC. This discovery provided evidence of the existence of Jerusalem's fortifications during the First Temple Period.

Third Sunday in Lent

GETHSEMANE: PRAYER AND OBEDIENCE

Scripture

Matthew 26:36–46; Luke 22:39–44

Going a little farther, he fell with his face to the ground and prayed, "My Father, if it is possible, may this cup be taken from me. Yet not as I will, but as you will."

—Matthew 26:39

And being in anguish, he prayed more earnestly, and his sweat was like drops of blood falling to the ground.

—Luke 22:44

Reflection

Twin themes set the tone for this week: prayer and obedience. The garden of Gethsemane is located just outside the Old City at the foot of the Mount of Olives. It is a place of immense historical and religious significance. It was where Jesus experienced his most profound moments of anguish and prayer before his crucifixion.

Today, Gethsemane remains a place of contemplation and prayer for pilgrims and visitors alike. The ancient olive trees, some of which are believed to be more than a thousand years old, create an atmosphere of quiet reflection. People from around the world come to this sacred place to meditate on the challenges and trials they face in their lives, seeking inspiration and strength from the example set by Jesus in his moments of deep spiritual struggle.

Prayer

Heavenly Father, thank you for the example of Jesus. Help us learn from his unwavering faith and surrender. Strengthen us in times of trial and enable us to trust in your perfect will. Forgive us for the times we have read about Gethsemane with dry eyes. We pray in the name of Jesus, who prayed, "not my will but thine." Amen.

MONDAY

Read Matthew 26:36–46 and Luke 22:39–44.

Matthew 26:36–46

Then Jesus went with his disciples to a place called Gethsemane, and he said to them, "Sit here while I go over there and pray." He took Peter and the two sons of Zebedee along with him, and he began to be sorrowful and troubled. Then he said to them, "My soul is overwhelmed with sorrow to the point of death. Stay here and keep watch with me."

Going a little farther, he fell with his face to the ground and prayed, "My Father, if it is possible, may this cup be taken from me. Yet not as I will, but as you will."

Then he returned to his disciples and found them sleeping. "Couldn't you men keep watch with me for one hour?" he asked Peter. "Watch and pray so that you will not fall into temptation. The spirit is willing, but the flesh is weak."

He went away a second time and prayed, "My Father, if it is not possible for this cup to be taken away unless I drink it, may your will be done."

When he came back, he again found them sleeping, because their eyes were heavy. So he left them and went away once more and prayed the third time, saying the same thing.

Then he returned to the disciples and said to them, "Are you still sleeping and resting? Look, the hour has come, and the Son of Man is delivered into the hands of sinners. Rise! Let us go! Here comes my betrayer!"

Luke 22:39–44

Jesus went out as usual to the Mount of Olives, and his disciples followed him. On reaching the place, he said to them, "Pray that you will not fall into temptation." He withdrew about a stone's throw beyond them, knelt down and prayed, "Father, if you are willing, take this cup from me; yet not my will, but yours be done." An angel from heaven appeared to him and strengthened him. And being in anguish, he prayed more earnestly, and his sweat was like drops of blood falling to the ground.

TUESDAY

Reflection

Historically, the garden of Gethsemane served as an agricultural space and an olive grove. The word "Gethsemane" itself derives from the Aramaic language meaning "oil press." This etymology highlights its connection to the production of olive oil, linking the garden to labor and sustenance, adding a layer of practical significance to its spiritual connotations. The name Gethsemane is significant because it symbolizes both the physical environment of the garden, which contained olive trees used for oil production, as well as the spiritual weight and pressure that Jesus endured during his time there. Picture the crushing of the olives as a symbol of the weight Jesus felt.

According to Matthew, Mark, and Luke, Jesus retreated to the garden with his disciples after the Passover meal. Knowing the imminent trials that awaited him, Jesus experienced great anguish and sorrow. In Gethsemane, Jesus prayed to God the Father, wrestling with the weight of his impending crucifixion and the sacrifice he was about to make for humanity. This moment is often referred to as "the agony in the garden."

The garden's meaning goes well beyond historical and biblical contexts. Its profound symbolism resonates with Christians throughout history. Gethsemane symbolizes the struggle between human frailty and divine purpose. Jesus's experience in the garden represents the human experience of wrestling with fear, doubt, and/or suffering, while also exemplifying the ultimate triumph of faith and obedience. It serves as a powerful reminder of the profound depths of Jesus's humanity and his unwavering commitment to fulfilling his divine mission. As fully human, he would have known the depth of human emotions and the weight of the sacrifice he was about to make. In the garden, he grappled with fear, sorrow, and the desire for another path. This moment makes his sacrifice even more meaningful and relatable to human experiences of struggle and doubt, and his resurrection even more powerful.

The garden also serves as an example of surrendering to God's plan, even in the face of immense personal suffering. Jesus's ultimate acceptance of his fate and his submission to God's will exemplify the profound faith and trust he had in his heavenly Father. In his prayer, Jesus uttered the words, "Father, if you are willing, take this cup from me; yet not my will, but yours be done" (Luke 22:42). This statement demonstrates the extent of Jesus's sacrifice, his complete obedience and surrender to God's plan. Thus, Jesus willingly took upon himself the sins of the world, setting in motion the events that led to his death and resurrection. This act of obedience and submission is considered the ultimate expression of God's love and grace toward humanity.

The actions and responses of the disciples in the garden are also significant. Despite Jesus's plea for them to keep watch, they fell asleep multiple times. Their failure to fully comprehend the weight of the moment, and their inability to support Jesus during his time of distress, highlight human frailty and the struggle to remain steadfast in faith. It serves as a reminder of the need for vigilance, dependence on God's strength, and empathy toward others in their times of need.

Visiting Gethsemane enables one to reflect on the themes of human struggle, divine redemption, and the transformative power of prayer, bringing renewed significance to Jesus's sacrifice and the enduring message of hope, love, and faith in the face of adversity.

For Additional Meditation

Psalm 44
Isaiah 41:1–10

Read these scriptures and consider how they relate to this week's Lenten themes of prayer and obedience, God's love for humanity, and God's desire to save humanity.

_____

_____

_____

_____

_____

_____

_____

WEDNESDAY

Reflection

Jesus, knowing what lay ahead—his arrest, torture, and crucifixion—entered the garden of Gethsemane with his disciples. He invited them to stay and pray while he pressed on a little farther. "Then Jesus went with his disciples to a place called Gethsemane, and he said to them, 'Sit here while I go over there and pray'" (Matthew 26:36). Falling to his knees, Jesus began to pour out his heart to his Father in fervent prayer. In this moment, we witness the humanity of Jesus in its rawest form. Aware of the excruciating path before him, his soul was deeply troubled. Luke's account tells us that his anguish was such that his sweat was like drops of blood. Yet, despite his agony, he uttered those profound words: "Yet not as I will, but as you will"(Matthew 26:39).

Note, first, that Gethsemane is a place of prayer. Few things signal our complete and utter dependence on God more than prayer. Prayer is an expression of our inability to meet the demands of life by ourselves. Prayer is a confession of our weakness, our frailty, our complete dependence on the sovereignty and provision of God. We acknowledge that we need his assistance, his strength, his enablement, and his sustaining grace.

Second, Gethsemane is a place of isolation. It's a curious thing, the way Jesus separated himself from the larger group of disciples and then, after inviting his three closest followers—Peter,

James, and John—to go on with him, he still separated himself from them too. As they moved into the Garden, the Lord opened his soul to them: "My soul is overwhelmed with sorrow to the point of death. Stay here and keep watch with me" (Matthew 26:38). He felt the need for the companionship of these disciples in his hour of trial, yet he still separated himself from them in order to be further isolated while he prayed.

Gethsemane is not only a place of prayer and isolation, but it is also a place of intense struggle. There is a battle going on here, a battle of the flesh against the spirit. It is a battle of the world against the kingdom of heaven. It is the battle of Satan against God. As Paul noted, "For our struggle is not against flesh and blood, but against the rulers, against the authorities, against the powers of this dark world and against the spiritual forces of evil in the heavenly realms" (Ephesians 6:12).

For Additional Meditation

Hebrews 10:19–24
Psalm 119:129–136

Read these scriptures and ponder how they relate to this week's themes of prayer and obedience, and Jesus's sacrifice for the sake of humanity.

_____

_____

_____

THURSDAY

Reflection

Gethsemane was where Jesus surrendered to the Father's will in the face of unimaginable suffering. His prayer that God's will be done, rather than his own, expresses a profound willingness to endure suffering for the sake of humanity's redemption. Gethsemane signifies the obedience and submission of Jesus to God's plan for salvation.

This act of submission highlights the core Christian message of self-sacrifice and the incredible love Jesus had for humanity. It also serves as a reminder to us of the importance of yielding to God's will, even when it involves personal sacrifice or hardship. In our lives, we often encounter trials, hardships, and overwhelming circumstances. In these moments we can learn from Jesus's unwavering faith and surrender.

This moment also assures us that, like Jesus, we can bring our concerns and burdens to God in prayer, pouring out our hearts honestly and sincerely. He understands our struggles, and his presence brings comfort and strength. Jesus, in his humanity, demonstrated that it is acceptable to express our deepest, scariest, most difficult emotions and fears to the Father. We can find solace knowing he is intimately acquainted with our pain.

Jesus's surrender also teaches us the significance of aligning our will with God's perfect plan. Despite his own desires, Jesus willingly submitted to the Father's purpose. He set aside his personal comfort and embraced the divine mission of redemption. In like manner, as followers of Jesus, we are called to submit our will to God's sovereign plan. It requires trust, faith, and a willingness to surrender our own desires and ambitions. We sometimes think of surrender as defeat. However, our surrender to God's will is a pathway to victory. It is in praying this same prayer—*not my will but yours be done*—that we triumph. When we surrender to God, we allow his purposes to take precedence over our own, opening the door to his blessings and the fulfillment of his plan for our lives.

As we reflect on Jesus's time in the garden of Gethsemane, may we be inspired by his unwavering example of faith and surrender. We too can and must be transparently honest with our heavenly Father in prayer, trusting in his wisdom. May God's grace always enable us to embrace his perfect will, even in the face of uncertainty and suffering.

For Additional Meditation

1 Corinthians 1:18–31
Hebrews 6:13–20

Read these scriptures and reflect on the idea that God and God's will are trustworthy.

FRIDAY

Ponder the words of this old familiar hymn as you continue to think on what you've studied and learned this week.

Take My Life, and Let It Be Consecrated (#455)

Take my life and let it be
Consecrated, Lord, to thee
Take my moments and my days
Let them flow in ceaseless praise
Let them flow in ceaseless praise

Take my hands and let them move
At the impulse of thy love
Take my feet and let them be
Swift and beautiful for thee
Swift and beautiful for thee

Take my voice and let me sing
Always, only, for my King
Take my lips and let them be
Filled with messages from thee
Filled with messages from thee

Take my silver and my gold
Not a mite would I withhold
Take my intellect and use
Every power as thou shalt choose
Every power as thou shalt choose

Take my will and make it thine
It shall be no longer mine
Take my heart—it is thine own
It shall be thy royal throne
It shall be thy royal throne

Take my love—my Lord, I pour
At thy feet its treasure store
Take myself—and I will be
Ever, only, all for thee
Ever, only, all for thee

SATURDAY IN JERUSALEM

The Western Wall, known also as the Wailing Wall, is an ancient structure located in the Old City. It holds tremendous religious, historical, and cultural significance for Jews worldwide. Understanding the historical context of the Western Wall is crucial in understanding its significance. The Jewish temple, constructed by King Herod the Great, was a center of religious and political life for the Jewish people. It was destroyed by the Romans following the Jewish revolt in 70 AD. The Western Wall is all that remains of the magnificent structure, serving as a tangible link to the Jewish people's ancient past.

The Wailing Wall is considered to be the holiest site in Judaism, attracting millions of visitors and worshipers each year. It is believed to be the closest accessible location to the Holy of Holies, the inner sanctum of the ancient temple. Jewish people from all over the world journey to the Western Wall to pray, especially during significant occasions such as Shabbat, festivals, and high holy days. Many believe that the wall acts as a channel to communicate directly with God and that prayers offered at this sacred site hold special significance.

The wall stands as an enduring symbol of the Jewish people's faith, history, and unity. As one gazes upon these weathered stones, it becomes evident that it is not merely a physical structure but a sacred space that has witnessed the countless prayers, tears, and hopes of generations who have sought solace and connection with God. Daily, thousands of prayers continue to be offered here. Many write their prayers and place them within the crevices of the wall.

Jill and I visited the wall several times during our stay. It seemed to have magnetic power. Anytime we were within the Old City, we could not leave without visiting the wall. Each time I stood before those towering ancient stones, I felt a sense of awe and reverence wash over me. Just a few days before we left for Jerusalem, I visited one of my college roommates who was in an intensive care unit, fighting for his life following a massive stroke. Just after arriving in the Old City, I learned he had passed. I immediately made my way to the wall to offer a prayer in his memory and for his wife.

The Western Wall is a visual and physical representation of the everlasting nature of God. Just as the stones have endured the passage of time, so does our faith in the Lord withstand the trials and challenges of life. In times of uncertainty, we can trust in the Lord, finding solace and strength in his unchanging love and presence. Our faith becomes an unyielding rock upon which we can stand and weather life's storms.

Leaving the Western Wall, one carries with them the profound sense of having been on holy ground. Its massive stones speak in silence, reminding worshipers of the power of faith, prayer, and trust. Whether spoken aloud or whispered silently, the prayers offered at the wall are imbued with deep sincerity and longing. It is a powerful reminder that God hears every prayer, understands every language, and responds to the yearnings of every heart.

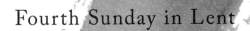

Fourth Sunday in Lent

PETER'S DENIAL: FACING FAILURE

Scripture

Mark 14:27–31; Luke 22:54–62

But Peter insisted emphatically, "Even if I have to die with you, I will never disown you." And all the others said the same.
—*Mark 14:31*

Reflection

The theme before us this week is facing failure. The landmark we visit is a modern-day church known simply as St. Peter in Gallicantu. Built in the twentieth century, it stands as a testament to the significance of this site. Designed by Italian architect Antonio Barluzzi, the church combines elements of Byzantine, Romanesque, and Crusader architectural styles. Situated on the eastern slope of Mount Zion, overlooking the Kidron Valley, this holy site is believed to be the location where Peter denied Jesus three times. The name "Gallicantu" is derived from the Latin word for "cock's crow," alluding to the biblical event.

St. Peter in Gallicantu serves as a reminder of human fallibility as well as the promise and possibility of redemption. It invites visitors to reflect on the frailties of human nature and the need for repentance and forgiveness. The site also offers a profound spiritual experience for Christians who seek to deepen their understanding of the biblical accounts and the life of the apostle Peter. The upper church houses beautiful stained-glass windows and mosaics that depict scenes from Peter's life.

Inside the church, visitors can explore various chapels and prayer spaces.

The history of St. Peter in Gallicantu dates back to the Byzantine period, around the fifth century AD, when a church was first built at the site. Over the centuries, the church has undergone various renovations and reconstructions, reflecting the changing architectural styles and the influence of different ruling powers in Jerusalem.

Prayer

Dear Savior, may you—who looked with compassion upon Peter at the point of his greatest failure—look our way too. Take our doubt and uncertainty and replace them with faith and confidence. Amen.

MONDAY

Read Mark 14:27–31 and Luke 22:54–62.

Mark 14:27–31

"You will all fall away," Jesus told them, "for it is written: 'I will strike the shepherd, and the sheep will be scattered.' But after I have risen, I will go ahead of you into Galilee."

Peter declared, "Even if all fall away, I will not."

"Truly I tell you," Jesus answered, "today—yes, tonight—before the rooster crows twice you yourself will disown me three times."

But Peter insisted emphatically, "Even if I have to die with you, I will never disown you." And all the others said the same.

Luke 22:54–62

Then seizing him, they led him away and took him into the house of the high priest. Peter followed at a distance. And when some there had kindled a fire in the middle of the courtyard and had sat down together, Peter sat down with them. A servant girl saw him seated there in the firelight. She looked closely at him and said, "This man was with him."

But he denied it. "Woman, I don't know him," he said.

A little later someone else saw him and said, "You also are one of them."

"Man, I am not!" Peter replied.

About an hour later another asserted, "Certainly this fellow was with him, for he is a Galilean."

Peter replied, "Man, I don't know what you're talking about!" Just as he was speaking, the rooster crowed. The Lord turned and looked straight at Peter. Then Peter remembered the word the Lord had spoken to him: "Before the rooster crows today, you will disown me three times." And he went outside and wept bitterly.

TUESDAY

Reflection

According to the Gospel accounts, Peter followed Jesus to the house of the high priest, Caiaphas, where Jesus was taken after his arrest in the garden of Gethsemane. In the courtyard of this house, Peter denied any association with Jesus three times before the rooster crowed, fulfilling Jesus's prophecy.

Today in the courtyard, there is a stunning sculpture motif depicting Peter's denial. The soldiers, the young servant girl, and a rooster surround a central figure who is in the process of denying that he knew Jesus. The scene is captivating. Inside, the main attraction is the Chapel of St. Peter, located on the lower level. The chapel contains an ancient staircase known as the Steps of Repentance. These steps, believed to be part of the original path leading to the high priest's palace, symbolize Peter's remorse and repentance after his denial of Jesus. Many pilgrims ascend and descend these steps in a symbolic act of seeking forgiveness and reconciliation.

Visitors can also explore the underground chambers thought to have been part of the palace. These chambers were discovered in the twentieth century during archaeological excavations. One chamber, called the Sacred Pit, is believed to have served as a holding place for prisoners, perhaps even including Jesus, before their trials.

One of the most significant moments of my time in Jerusalem was visiting this site and descending into the pit. On one hand, I was speechless as I tried to imagine Jesus being lowered into this deep, dark hole. On the other hand, I felt an immense sense of praise and thanksgiving. While I was there in the pit, others joined me and quietly began to sing the third verse of "How Great Thou Art." It was a such a powerful moment that I joined them, and we had to sing through our tears.

And when I think, that God, his Son not sparing
Sent him to die, I scarce can take it in
That on the cross, my burden gladly bearing
He bled and died to take away my sin.

Then sings my soul, my Savior God, to thee
How great thou art! How great thou art!
Then sings my soul, my Savior God, to thee
How great thou art! How great thou art!

For Additional Meditation

Ephesians 6:10–20
James 1:2–15
Jude 1:24–25

Consider how these scriptures speak to our tendency to fail, as well as what we can do to protect ourselves from temptation, how we respond following failure, and God's role in all of it.

WEDNESDAY

Reflection

In the courtyard, Peter found himself trapped between love and fear. He didn't want to leave because he loved the Lord. Yet at the same time, he did not want his identity to be discovered because he feared for his own safety. He continued to hang around, trying not to be noticed, as he joined the small group huddled by the fire.

It is interesting to note the progression of Peter's denials. First, remember that Peter is the one who proclaimed, "You are the Messiah, the son of the living God" (Matthew 16:16). Peter often referred to Jesus as "master." He also called him "Lord." But in his moment of failure, during his third denial, he referred to Jesus as simply "this man you're talking about," while swearing and calling down curses (Mark 14:71). To call down curses does not mean Peter used a string of vulgarities to emphasize his point. It means he was invoking a curse upon himself if what he was saying was untrue—even though he knew it was untrue! At the very moment when Jesus needed him, Peter—who promised never to fall away even if everyone else did—was emphatically denying he ever knew Jesus.

Luke's account of this story contains one detail the others omit. Luke 22:61 says that when the rooster crowed, "the Lord turned and looked straight at Peter." Since this was the middle of the night, it must have happened just as the guards were taking Jesus from his interview with Caiaphas to his trial before the Sanhedrin. By this time, Jesus's face was perhaps already black and blue, his eyes almost swollen shut, his cheeks bruised and covered with spittle. Even though it is the dead of night, Peter could see him perfectly in the firelight. And Jesus could see Peter perfectly.

Jesus didn't say a word. He simply looked at Peter, who had denied him for the third time. Everything happened just as the Lord predicted.

I wonder what was in that look Jesus gave Peter. Conviction? Condemnation? Disappointment? Hurt? Maybe, but I am more inclined to believe it was a look of compassion.

For Additional Meditation

Hebrews 13:20–21
Ephesians 3:16–19
Romans 8:18–39

Consider these scriptures in light of Peter's failure and reflect on what they have to say to us today in light of our own failures.

THURSDAY

Reflection

At the moment the rooster crowed, Peter was a broken man—yet things that are broken can be repaired. A broken bone often becomes stronger after it heals. Something that occurs during the healing process can actually make the break point stronger than it was before. The same thing is true of our failures. God can take us when we are broken and make us stronger than we were before. Though we may stumble, this dark moment in the life of Peter assures us that, by God's grace, we can be restored. That's what happened to Peter.

The Gospel of John records the moment of his restoration in chapter 21 when the Lord appeared to his disciples on the shore of the Sea of Galilee. Peter's guilt was met with grace; his shame with sympathy; his failure with the faithfulness of God. Before his failure, he was loud, boisterous, unreliable. Afterward, Peter became a bold preacher of the gospel. Before, he talked too much about himself; afterward he talked only of what Jesus could do for others. He was the same man, but he was different. Following this moment, Peter's vanity, pride, self-confidence, impulsiveness, and unreliability dissipated—replaced with a new level of humility, confidence in God, courage, and boldness coupled with a renewed determination to serve Jesus Christ.

One of the central themes of the season of Lent is the recognition of our human frailty, including those moments of spiritual failure we may experience. Peter's denial of Jesus offers us several points of potential application for our own lives.

1. Human Weakness. Peter's denial reminds us that even the most dedicated and faithful individuals can succumb to fear and doubt. This reality underscores the human condition and our need for humility in acknowledging our own imperfections.

2. Inattentiveness. Peter talked when he should have been listening. At the Passover meal, when Jesus said all his disciples would desert him, Peter impulsively blurted out, "Even if everyone else does that, I never will!" Within six hours, Peter would come to regret those brave words. He *heard*, but he did not *listen*. He was self-assured and thus unaware of the circumstances in which he might find himself.

3. Humility and Pride. Peter's denial also highlights the destructive nature of pride. Peter must have felt ashamed and humiliated when Jesus looked at him after the rooster crowed. When we embrace humility, we recognize that our strength comes from God rather than our own abilities.

4. Vigilance in Faith. Peter's failure serves as a warning about the dangers of complacency and overconfidence in our faith. Peter still ended up denying Jesus despite his strong declaration of loyalty. We need to remain vigilant in our faith and continually seek spiritual growth.

5. Peer Pressure. Peter's denial was partly a result of the pressure he felt from those around him. Peer pressure and societal norms can influence the choices we make each day. We must learn to resist negative influences and stand firm in our beliefs.

6. Repentance and Forgiveness. After his denial, Peter experienced profound remorse, and he repented of his actions. Genuine repentance is important in the life of a Christian because it will lead to forgiveness in Christ. No matter how grave our mistakes, there is always hope for redemption through sincere repentance.

7. The Unwavering Love of Christ. Despite Peter's denial, Jesus never stopped loving him because Christ offers unconditional love and forgiveness. This reminder is a source of comfort and encouragement for any who may feel unworthy.

8. Courage and Witness. Peter went on to become a courageous witness for Christ, preaching the gospel fearlessly. Failure does not have to define us. God can use our weakness for God's glory.

9. Learning from Mistakes. Mistakes and failures can be valuable opportunities for growth and learning. Like Peter, we can use our past errors as stepping stones toward greater faith and maturity.

Peter's denial of Jesus speaks to any who find themselves in a situation where they are tempted to turn away from the Lord or deny their faith. If or when that happens, Peter's experience can be instructive. This story is for those who are tempted or who have already fallen because this story does not end with the denial. The Lord is understanding and compassionate toward Peter and will be toward us as well. Peter's is a hope-filled story. If he can fall, anybody can. Yet at the same time, if Peter can come back, anybody can!

For Additional Meditation

1 Peter 1:3–16
Isaiah 50:7–10

Reflect on the way these scriptures speak to the way God loves and redeems us when we fail. Although the authorship of 1 Peter is not unanimously agreed on among scholars, imagine when you read the 1 Peter passage that it *was* written by Peter. How does the context of Peter's own personal experience of failure and redemption add meaning to these words?

_____

_____

_____

_____

_____

_____

_____

_____

_____

_____

_____

_____

_____

_____

_____

_____

_____

_____

_____

_____

_____

_____

_____

FRIDAY

Ponder the words of these old familiar hymns as you continue to think on what you've studied and learned this week.

Just As I Am (#343)

Just as I am without one plea
But that thy blood was shed for me
And that thou bidd'st me come to thee
O Lamb of God, I come! I come!

Just as I am, tho' tossed about
With many a conflict, many a doubt
Fightings and fears within, without
O Lamb of God, I come! I come!

Hiding in Thee (#558)

In the calm of the noontide, in sorrow's lone hour
In times when temptation casts o'er me its pow'r
In the tempests of life, on its wide, heaving sea
Thou blest Rock of Ages, I'm hiding in thee
Hiding in thee, hiding in thee
Thou blest Rock of Ages, I'm hiding in thee

SATURDAY IN JERUSALEM

With its rich history, vibrant culture, and stunning scenery, Jerusalem is a city that continues to amaze and inspire visitors from all over the world. The Old City, a UNESCO World Heritage site, is a microcosm of cultural, religious, and historical significance. With a history spanning nearly four thousand years, this ancient city is divided into four distinct sections: the Jewish Quarter, the Christian Quarter, the Muslim Quarter, and the Armenian Quarter. Each section represents a unique mixture of traditions, architecture, and religious devotion. Together, they encapsulate the city's significance as a symbol of coexistence and shared heritage. Exploring the quarters allows visitors to witness the intertwining threads of religious devotion, cultural tradition, and historical legacy.

Understanding and appreciating the significance of each quarter contributes to preserving the essence of Jerusalem, honoring its place as a global heritage site, and embracing the city's past while hopefully fostering a more harmonious future.

The Jewish Quarter

The Jewish Quarter is situated in the southeastern corner of the Old City and is the heart of Jewish life in Jerusalem. With every step, one encounters the rich saga of Jewish history, culture, and spirituality. For millennia, this quarter has served as a focal point for Jewish life, embodying the resilience, tenacity, and profound connection of the Jewish people to their ancestral homeland. Walking through the streets of the Jewish Quarter reveals a captivating blend of ancient tradition, religious devotion, architectural marvel, and a vibrant community that breathes life into the heart of Jerusalem. Dating back to biblical times, the Jewish Quarter has witnessed the rise and fall of empires, the destruction and rebuilding of the holy temple, and the trials and tribulations of the Jewish people. The Western Wall, a sacred remnant of the second temple, is the centerpiece of the quarter and serves as a symbol of Jewish faith and perseverance.

As Jill and I explored the narrow alleyways and courtyards of the Jewish Quarter, we encountered a stunning array of architectural wonders. The Hurva Synagogue, a magnificent structure with an iconic dome and intricate decorations, stands as a symbol of Jewish revival and determination. Restored to its former glory after being destroyed and rebuilt multiple times, the synagogue radiates a unique blend of past and present.

The Jewish Quarter pulsates with religious life and spirituality. The *yeshivas* (Jewish seminaries) within the quarter are centers of Jewish scholarship where students engage in the study of Torah and the preservation of ancient traditions. The Jewish Quarter is also home to the revered Ramban Synagogue and Tiferet Yisrael Synagogue, each offering a unique opportunity for prayer, reflection, and connection.

Beyond its historical and religious importance, the Jewish Quarter exudes a cultural vibrance that is woven into the fabric of daily life. Art galleries showcase contemporary and traditional art, capturing the essence of Jewish identity and heritage. Restaurants and cafes offer a range of kosher cuisine from traditional dishes passed down through generations to innovative creations that reflect modern influence. The Jewish Quarter thrives as a close-knit community, with residents sharing a strong sense of belonging and pride in their heritage. The small, vibrant neighborhoods are home to families who have inhabited these streets for generations, fostering a deep-rooted connection to their ancestors and a collective commitment to preserving their unique way of life.

This area boasts a blend of ancient ruins, including the Cardo, a reconstructed Roman-era market street. The term "cardo" refers to the main north-south street in a Roman city or military camp. In the context of the Old City, the Cardo once ran through the city during the Roman and Byzantine periods. It was a wide, colonnaded street that stretched from the Damascus Gate in the north to the Zion Gate in the south, dividing the city into two sections.

The Jewish Quarter's timeless streets carry the weight of centuries of Jewish resilience, devotion, and aspiration. From the sacred Western Wall to the architectural wonders, religious institutions, and rich community life, the Jewish Quarter is a testament to the enduring presence and perseverance of the Jewish people in their ancestral homeland. It stands as an emblem of hope, reminding visitors of the indomitable spirit of a people connected to their past and their future, forever entwined within the heart of Jerusalem.

The Christian Quarter

The Christian Quarter, located in the northwest of the Old City, obviously holds immense meaning for Christians worldwide. Pilgrims from various Christian traditions visit this quarter to partake in religious ceremonies and connect with the roots of their faith. The Christian Quarter's winding alleyways reveal churches, monasteries, and traditional markets, providing a glimpse into the vibrant and diverse Christian heritage of the city.

The Christian Quarter is home to numerous iconic religious sites, including the Church of the Holy Sepulchre, which stands as the paramount symbol of Christianity and the focal point of the quarter's spiritual significance. This church is believed to encompass both the site of Jesus's crucifixion (Golgotha) and his burial tomb. Pilgrims from around the world come to pay homage to these sacred spaces, immersing themselves in the history and devotion that resonate within the hallowed walls. The church's architectural magnificence—ornate chapels, stunning mosaics, and dimly lit corridors—creates an atmosphere of reverence and awe. Adjacent to the Church of the Holy Sepulchre are bustling, narrow, cobbled streets that wind their way through a lively marketplace filled with shops, cafes, and stalls selling religious artifacts, icons, and souvenirs.

Beyond the area around the Church of the Holy Sepulchre, the Christian Quarter boasts a multitude of other important sites. The *Via Dolorosa* meanders through the quarter, marked by the Stations of the Cross. Pilgrims and visitors can retrace the footsteps of Jesus, reflecting on his journey and the significance of his sacrifice.

Other notable sites include the Church of St. Anne, known for its exceptional acoustics and serene courtyard; and the Church of the Flagellation, commemorating the scourging of Jesus before his crucifixion. These sites offer glimpses into the biblical events that unfolded in this area and give visitors an opportunity to connect with the profound history and spirituality embedded in every corner.

The Muslim Quarter

The Muslim Quarter, occupying the northeastern part of the Old City, is the largest and most populous. Stretching from the Damascus Gate in the north to the Western Wall in the south, the Muslim Quarter's busy streets are lined with markets, shops, and traditional architecture. Entering visitors are immediately enveloped in a sensory feast. The air is filled with the aroma of spices and traditional Middle Eastern delicacies, while the sound of merchants haggling with customers creates an energetic atmosphere.

The most iconic site in the Muslim Quarter is the Dome of the Rock in the Al-Aqsa compound. It is one of the oldest and largest mosques in the world. Its intricate mosaics and stunning calligraphy make it a true masterpiece of Islamic art and architecture. This sprawling complex encompasses not only the mosque but also beautiful courtyards, gardens, and historical structures. It is believed to be the location of the prophet Muhammad's night journey from Mecca to Jerusalem. Its grandeur and historical importance make it a site of pilgrimage and worship for Muslims worldwide.

In addition to its architectural wonders and bustling markets, the Muslim Quarter is home to a varied population that reflects the complex and multifaceted nature of Jerusalem. Arab Muslims form the majority, but the quarter also houses a significant number of Christian and Armenian residents. This diversity is reflected in the varied places of worship, cultural institutions, and culinary offerings within the quarter. It serves as a living testament to the coexistence and intermingling of different religious and cultural traditions throughout Jerusalem's history.

The Armenian Quarter

The Armenian Quarter, located in the southwestern corner of the Old City, covers a relatively small area but is rich in historical and cultural significance. The Armenians have a longstanding connection to Jerusalem dating back to the fourth century AD, when Armenia became the first nation to adopt Christianity as its state religion. Pilgrims and monks from Armenia made their way to the Holy Land, establishing monasteries and religious institutions in Jerusalem. Over time, an Armenian community took root, finding solace in the holy sites and establishing their presence within the city walls.

It is home to several key landmarks, including the St. James Cathedral, also known as the Armenian Patriarchate, which serves as the spiritual and administrative center for the Armenian Orthodox Church. The cathedral's striking architecture, adorned with intricate carvings and beautiful artwork, is a testament to the deep religious devotion of the Armenian community. The Armenian section also houses St. Mark's Chapel, the Chapel of the Ascension, and the Chapel of St. Helena, each associated with biblical events and revered by both Armenian and Christian pilgrims. The narrow streets of the Armenian Quarter wind their way through ancient stone buildings, creating an atmosphere that transports visitors back in time.

Despite their relatively small numbers, the Armenian community has played an integral role in developing Jerusalem's diverse society. They have contributed to the city's economic life through businesses, crafts, and tourism. Moreover, the Armenians have actively participated in interfaith dialogue, promoting understanding and cooperation among different religious communities in Jerusalem. Through their deep-rooted connection to the city's history, their commitment to preserving their heritage, and their contributions to the cultural and economic landscape, the Armenians have left an indelible mark on Jerusalem.

Fifth Sunday in Lent

VIA DOLOROSA: THE WAY OF SUFFERING

Scripture

Matthew 27:22–31; Mark 15:37–41

They stripped him and put a scarlet robe on him, and then twisted together a crown of thorns and set it on his head. They put a staff in his right hand. Then they knelt in front of him and mocked him. "Hail, king of the Jews!" they said. They spit on him, and took the staff and struck him on the head again and again.
—*Matthew 27:28–30*

Reflection

Via Dolorosa—meaning "Way of Suffering" or "Way of Sorrows" in Latin—is a historic and significant route that winds its way through the Old City of Jerusalem. It is believed to be the path Jesus traveled while carrying his cross to the site of his crucifixion. Walking the *Via Dolorosa* can be a deeply meaningful and spiritual experience for those who want to retrace the steps of Jesus. The Bible does not specifically mention the *Via Dolorosa* by name. However, we know from Scripture that Jesus carried his cross, with help from Simon of Cyrene, from the Praetorium where the soldiers mocked and beat him to the site on Mount Calvary (or Golgotha) where he was crucified.

The *Via Dolorosa* that can be followed today is marked by fourteen stations, each noting a particular event or episode that occurred or is said to have occurred during Jesus's final journey. These stations are marked by chapels, monuments, and plaques and are visited by thousands every year. The stations begin at the Antonia Fortress, where Jesus was condemned to death, and end at the Church of the Holy Sepulchre, believed to be the site of his crucifixion, burial, and resurrection. This modern path, and its name, were created in the fourteenth century by Franciscan monks looking for something to call the stretch of road along which Christ walked under the weight of the cross. Although the modern *Via Dolorosa* and the fourteen stations are not specifically grounded in Scripture, they are nonetheless helpful in imagining the arduous trek Jesus made on his way to the cross.

To walk slowly along the *Via Dolorosa* is a deeply spiritual experience that calls us to reflect on the depth of Christ's love, the weight of our sins, and the power of faith. It has become a pilgrimage site for believers seeking to follow the footsteps of Jesus in the midst of his suffering. The walk enables believers to connect with the story of Jesus in a tangible way, serving as a powerful reminder of Jesus's humanity and his willingness to endure immense pain for the sake of others.

Prayer

Gracious Lord, as we contemplate the Via Dolorosa, *we stand in awe of your immeasurable love and sacrifice. Help us carry our own crosses with faith and resilience, knowing you are with us, step by step, in every trial. Thank you for your sustaining grace. May we live our lives as a reflection of your journey along the way of suffering. Amen.*

MONDAY

Read Matthew 27:22–31 and Mark 15:37–41.

Matthew 27:22–31

"What shall I do, then, with Jesus who is called the Messiah?" Pilate asked.

They all answered, "Crucify him!"

"Why? What crime has he committed?" asked Pilate.

But they shouted all the louder, "Crucify him!"

When Pilate saw that he was getting nowhere, but that instead an uproar was starting, he took water and washed his hands in front of the crowd. "I am innocent of this man's blood," he said. "It is your responsibility!"

All the people answered, "His blood is on us and on our children!"

Then he released Barabbas to them. But he had Jesus flogged, and handed him over to be crucified.

Then the governor's soldiers took Jesus into the Praetorium and gathered the whole company of soldiers around him. They stripped him and put a scarlet robe on him, and then twisted together a crown of thorns and set it on his head. They put a staff in his right hand. Then they knelt in front of him and mocked him. "Hail, king of the Jews!" they said. They spit on him, and took the staff and struck him on the head again and again. After they had mocked him, they took off the robe and put his own clothes on him. Then they led him away to crucify him.

Mark 15:37–41

With a loud cry, Jesus breathed his last.

The curtain of the temple was torn in two from top to bottom. And when the centurion, who stood there in front of Jesus, saw how he died, he said, "Surely this man was the Son of God!"

Some women were watching from a distance. Among them were Mary Magdalene, Mary the mother of James the younger and of Joseph, and Salome. In Galilee these women had followed him and cared for his needs. Many other women who had come up with him to Jerusalem were also there.

TUESDAY

Reflection

The journey along the *Via Dolorosa* invites Jesus followers to encounter the physical and emotional pain he endured for our sake. Each station tells a story of selflessness, compassion, and unyielding love. The description of the various stations occasionally varies, depending on the specific theological and cultural tradition. Today, reflect on the first seven stations.

Station 1: Jesus Is Condemned to Death

Located in the Antonia Fortress, this station marks the moment when Pontius Pilate pronounced Jesus guilty and condemned him to death.

Station 2: Jesus Carries His Cross

This spot commemorates the placing of the cross on Jesus's back as he began the physical journey toward his crucifixion.

Station 3: Jesus Falls the First Time

At this station, pilgrims are encouraged to reflect on Jesus's first fall under the weight of the cross. It is believed to have occurred near the entrance to what is now the Church of the Flagellation.

Station 4: Jesus Meets His Mother

Tradition suggests this is where Jesus encountered his mother, Mary. It takes place close to the Church of St. Anne.

Station 5: Simon of Cyrene Helps Jesus Carry the Cross

This stop provides a place to contemplate the moment when Simon of Cyrene was pressed into service to carry Jesus's cross for him.

Station 6: Veronica Wipes the Face of Jesus

This station symbolizes a compassionate act that is not described in Scripture but is part of several Christian traditions. Here, according to legend, a woman named Veronica used her veil to wipe the blood and sweat from Jesus's face.

Station 7: Jesus Falls the Second Time

At this place, pilgrims remember Jesus falling a second time beneath the burden of the cross, near the entrance to what is now the Coptic Orthodox Patriarchate.

For Additional Meditation

Psalm 23
John 10:1–18

As you contemplate the suffering of Jesus, consider the ways we also suffer in our own lives, and read these scriptures that promise God's comfort.

WEDNESDAY

Reflection

Today, consider the final seven stations of the cross that Christian pilgrims can visit along the modern *Via Dolorosa*.

Station 8: Jesus Encounters the Women of Jerusalem

This location symbolizes Jesus's encounter with the women of Jerusalem, who mourned his impending crucifixion.

Station 9: Jesus Falls the Third Time

At this point along the way, visitors are encouraged to reflect on Jesus's third and final fall before reaching Calvary. It is near the Greek Orthodox Patriarchate.

Station 10: Jesus Is Stripped of His Garments

Here, pilgrims are to recall how the soldiers stripped Jesus of his garments before nailing him to the cross. The site is situated near the Armenian Catholic Patriarchate.

Station 11: Jesus Is Nailed to the Cross

This is a place to contemplate the agonizing moment when Jesus was nailed to the cross. It is found within the courtyard of the Holy Sepulchre.

Station 12: Jesus Dies on the Cross

Here, visitors reflect on Jesus's ultimate sacrifice in the crucifixion. This station is inside the Holy Sepulchre.

Station 13: Jesus Is Taken Down from the Cross

Also located within the Holy Sepulchre, this station represents the sorrowful moment when Jesus's lifeless body was taken down from the cross.

Station 14: Jesus Is Laid in the Tomb

The final station, still within the Holy Sepulchre, marks the burial of Jesus. It is a place of profound reverence and contemplation.

Some add a fifteenth station to acknowledge the immense significance of the resurrection, but this station is not traditionally included in Stations of the Cross observances around the world, nor does a marking for it appear on the modern *Via Dolorosa*.

For Additional Meditation

Luke 12:22–34
Psalm 121

Jesus himself was intimately familiar with the Hebrew Scriptures. As you reflect on the second half of his suffering journey, read also these scriptures today and consider his faithfulness to God's will, God's faithfulness to him, and God's faithfulness to us.

_____

_____

_____

_____

_____

_____

_____

_____

_____

_____

_____

_____

_____

_____

THURSDAY

Reflection

The *Via Dolorosa* has become a pathway of introspection for those who visit today. Walking the *Via Dolorosa* is an experiential and sensory journey. As one walks along the route, he or she can touch ancient stones, observe intricate details, and interact with the local community, fostering a profound connection with the historical and religious heritage of Jerusalem. The mingling scents of incense, the echo of prayers, and the hushed tones of worshipers create an ambiance that transports visitors to a different time and place, evoking a sense of reverence and awe.

This winding path is a reminder of the Lord's sacrifice, suffering, and shame. Since his arrest in the garden, Jesus had not slept. He was questioned on four separate occasions with no wrongdoing discovered. He was beaten severely by the temple guards as well as mocked, beaten, and flogged by the Roman guards. Then, having received a death sentence, he was forced to carry his cross in public through the streets of the city. What shines through the suffering and shame is a powerful demonstration of the selflessness of the Savior. He laid down his life for us! The good shepherd laid down his life for the sheep (see John 10).

Jesus bore our sins, carrying the weight of the world's transgressions upon his shoulders. He endured mockery, humiliation, and excruciating pain—all because of his immeasurable love for us. The *Via Dolorosa* can be a powerful reminder that our own journey may be marked by moments of suffering as well. As we consider the way of suffering, we are reminded that we can find the strength to endure in Christ. We do not carry our burdens alone, for Jesus is always *at* our side and *on* our side, every step of the way. Remember that one need not actually be in Jerusalem to observe the journey of the *Via Dolorosa*. In reading the scriptures and thinking about the way of the cross, we can be personally reminded of the significance of Christ's sacrifice.

For Additional Meditation

Isaiah 49:8–18
Psalm 103:1–13

Consider what these Hebrew scriptures would've meant to those who experienced the life and death of Jesus firsthand. Would their meaning or significance have changed at all for the people of God, following Jesus's death? What about after the resurrection?

_____

_____

_____

_____

_____

_____

_____

_____

_____

_____

_____

_____

_____

_____

FRIDAY

Ponder the words of these old familiar hymns as you continue to think on what you've studied and learned this week.

O Sacred Head, Now Wounded (#249)

O sacred Head, now wounded, with grief and shame weighed down
Now scornfully surrounded with thorns, thine only crown
O sacred Head, what glory, what bliss till now was thine
Yet, though despised and gory, I joy to call thee mine

What thou, my Lord, hast suffered was all for sinners' gain
Mine, mine was the transgression, but thine the deadly pain
Lo, here I fall, my Savior! 'Tis I deserve thy place
Look on me with thy favor and grant me to thy grace

Were You There? (#250)

Were you there when they crucified my Lord?
Were you there when they crucified my Lord?
O, sometimes it causes me to tremble, tremble, tremble!
Were you there when they crucified my Lord?

Were you there when they nailed him to a tree?
Were you there when they nailed him to a tree?
O, sometimes it causes me to tremble, tremble, tremble!
Were you there when they nailed him to a tree?

Were you there when they laid him in a tomb?
Were you there when they laid him in a tomb?
O, sometimes it causes me to tremble, tremble, tremble!
Were you there when they laid him in a tomb?

Were you there when he rose up from the dead?
Were you there when he rose up from the dead?
O, sometimes it causes me to tremble, tremble, tremble!
Were you there when he rose up from the dead?

SATURDAY IN JERUSALEM

The Damascus Gate, at the center of the north wall, is one of the busiest gates to the Old City. Like all the other gates, it too stands as a magnificent testament to the city's rich history and cultural heritage. As one of the main entrances to Jerusalem's Old City, the Damascus Gate is a focal point for locals and visitors alike.

The origins of the Damascus Gate can be traced back more than two thousand years to the time of the Roman Empire. Constructed during the reign of Roman Emperor Hadrian in the second century CE, it was part of a grand urban development project that aimed to transform Jerusalem into a Roman city known as Aelia Capitolina. The gate's location was strategically chosen on the road leading to Damascus, hence its name.

The area around the Damascus Gate has served as a melting pot, where the traditions and customs of various civilizations have intermingled. The gate's bustling marketplace has attracted people from different backgrounds, fostering social and economic interactions and becoming a microcosm of Jerusalem's cultural diversity.

The Damascus Gate has religious importance as well. For Christians, it is associated with the *Via Dolorosa*, the path believed to be taken by Jesus during his crucifixion. Jews revere the gate as the closest point of access to the Western Wall, their holiest site. Muslims consider the gate a vital entrance to the Al-Aqsa Mosque, the third-holiest site in Islam.

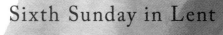

Sixth Sunday in Lent

GOLGOTHA AND THE TOMB: THE SEVEN LAST WORDS

Scripture

Luke 23:33–34; Luke 23:39–43; John 19:25–27; Matthew 27:45–46; John 19:28–30; Luke 23:44–46

Jesus called out with a loud voice, "Father, into your hands I commit my spirit." When he had said this, he breathed his last.
—*Luke 23:46*

Reflection

The focus of this final stop on the Lenten journey is on the last words of Jesus from the cross. The landmarks are the Church of the Holy Sepulchre and the Garden Tomb. Both are claimed as the sites of Jesus's crucifixion, burial, and resurrection.

The Church of the Holy Sepulchre, situated in the Christian Quarter of Jerusalem's Old City, draws countless pilgrims each year. The church's architecture is a testament to its rich history. The origins of the Church of the Holy Sepulchre can be traced back to the reign of Emperor Constantine the Great. In the early fourth century, Constantine's mother, Helena, traveled to Jerusalem and identified the sites associated with Jesus's crucifixion and burial. Constantine ordered the construction of a church complex over these sites. The church was consecrated in 335 AD.

Over the centuries, the church has undergone various modifications, expansions, and renovations. These changes were often influenced by different Christian traditions and the political rulers of Jerusalem. The Byzantines, Persians, Arabs, and Crusaders all had a hand in shaping the church's appearance. During the Muslim conquest of Jerusalem in 638, the Church of the Holy Sepulchre came under Islamic control. It was spared from destruction but underwent significant changes. The church also suffered damage during the various battles and sieges of Jerusalem during the Crusades. The Crusaders took control of Jerusalem in the twelfth century and did a major renovation and reconstruction of the church. Years later, during the Ottoman Empire's rule over Jerusalem, the church was again subjected to neglect and disrepair. Various Christian denominations struggled to maintain their rights and responsibilities over the church. In the nineteenth century, a status-quo agreement to manage and maintain the church was reached among the groups (including the Roman Catholic Church, Greek Orthodox Church, and Armenian Apostolic Church, among others). This agreement is still in place today.

The structure of the church consists of various chapels and sections, each associated with a specific event in the life of Jesus. For example, the Stone of Anointing, where Jesus's body is said to have been prepared for burial, stands as one of several focal points of devotion. The church is also home to sites like the Chapel of St. Helena, where the true cross is believed to have been found. The main focal point is called the Aedicule, a small structure that encloses the Holy Sepulchre. This chamber is believed to be the tomb where Jesus's body was laid to rest and from which he rose on the third day. Pilgrims from all over the world visit the Aedicule to offer prayers, meditate, and seek spiritual solace.

In more recent times, another site, called the Garden Tomb, has been identified as the possible place of crucifixion and burial. British army officer and amateur archaeologist Charles George Gordon identified this tomb in 1867 as a possible location for the burial of Jesus based on its proximity to what appears to be a skull-shaped outcropping (Golgotha) just beyond the Damascus Gate. Following Gordon's identification of this spot, the Garden Tomb gained popularity particularly among Protestants. In 1894, a British organization called the Garden Tomb Association was formed to oversee the preservation and maintenance of the site. The association has since worked to maintain the garden's appearance and provide a peaceful place for reflection and worship.

The Garden Tomb is characterized by a rock-cut tomb that resembles the description of the tomb in the New Testament. It is surrounded by a beautiful garden area with pathways and benches for visitors to explore and contemplate. At this site, individuals and groups gather for prayer, reflection, and Communion, particularly during the Easter season.

Most visitors to Jerusalem make their way to both sites because we acknowledge that the exact location cannot be known for sure. Nonetheless, one must remember that the overriding significance does not rest in the *where* of the death of Christ but in the *fact* of it. The fact that the tomb is empty is what matters.

Prayer

(from the PCUSA *Book of Common Worship*)

O God, you gave your only Son to suffer death on the cross for our redemption. You delivered us from the power of death. Grant us so to die daily to sin, that we may evermore live with him in the joy of his resurrection; through Jesus Christ our Lord, who lives and reigns with you and the Holy Spirit, one God, now and forever. Amen.

MONDAY

Read Luke 23:33–34; Luke 23:39–43; John 19:25–27; Matthew 27:45–46; John 19:28–30; and Luke 23:44–46.

1. Luke 23:33–34

When they came to the place called the Skull, they crucified him there, along with the criminals—one on his right, the other on his left. Jesus said, "Father, forgive them, for they do not know what they are doing." And they divided up his clothes by casting lots.

2. Luke 23:39–43

One of the criminals who hung there hurled insults at him: "Aren't you the Messiah? Save yourself and us!"

But the other criminal rebuked him. "Don't you fear God," he said, "since you are under the same sentence? We are punished justly, for we are getting what our deeds deserve. But this man has done nothing wrong."

Then he said, "Jesus, remember me when you come into your kingdom."

Jesus answered him, "Truly I tell you, today you will be with me in paradise."

3. John 19:25–27

Near the cross of Jesus stood his mother, his mother's sister, Mary the wife of Clopas, and Mary Magdalene. When Jesus saw his mother there, and the disciple whom he loved standing nearby, he said to her, "Woman, here is your son," and to the disciple, "Here is your mother." From that time on, this disciple took her into his home.

4. Matthew 27:45–46

From noon until three in the afternoon darkness came over all the land. About three in the afternoon Jesus cried out in a loud voice, "Eli, Eli, lema sabachthani?" *(which means "My God, my God, why have you forsaken me?").*

5 & 6. John 19:28–30

Later, knowing that everything had now been finished, and so that Scripture would be fulfilled, Jesus said, "I am thirsty." A jar of wine vinegar was there, so they soaked a sponge in it, put the sponge on a stalk of the hyssop plant, and lifted it to Jesus' lips. When he had received the drink, Jesus said, "It is finished." With that, he bowed his head and gave up his spirit.

7. Luke 23:44–46

It was now about noon, and darkness came over the whole land until three in the afternoon, for the sun stopped shining. And the curtain of the temple was torn in two. Jesus called out with a loud voice, "Father, into your hands I commit my spirit." When he had said this, he breathed his last.

TUESDAY

Reflection

All four Gospels give similar yet unique accounts of Jesus's crucifixion and death. When we look at them together, we can collect seven final statements that Jesus made while he was on the cross before he died. These are traditionally called the "seven last words." These statements are significant for several reasons.

1. Expression of Jesus's Humanity and Divinity

The seven last words provide insight into both the humanity and divinity of Jesus. They show his physical suffering and emotional anguish as he endured the crucifixion, while also highlighting his divine nature as the Son of God.

2. Teachings and Messages

Each of the seven statements conveys a unique teaching or message.

3. Redemption and Forgiveness

More than one of Jesus's statements from the cross emphasize redemption and forgiveness, underscoring God's boundless mercy and the possibility of reconciliation with God.

4. Abandonment and Desolation

In his cry to God about being forsaken, Jesus expresses a sense of abandonment and desolation, reflecting his unique role as the bearer of humanity's sins and the separation he felt from God during this crucial moment.

5. Triumphant Conclusion

The final statements that Jesus makes as he dies ("It is finished" or "Into your hands I commit my spirit," depending on which Gospel you're reading) signify the ultimate act of obedience to God's plan and victory over sin and death. Jesus declares that his earthly mission is complete and anticipates his resurrection.

6. Reflection and Contemplation

The seven last words provide a framework for meditation, prayer, and reflection for Christians, particularly during Holy Week and Good Friday. It is not unusual for Good Friday services to center on these statements from the cross, thus encouraging believers to contemplate the significance of Jesus's sacrifice.

7. Unity among Christians

Finally, the seven last words also serve as a common point of theological reflection and devotion, bringing together Christians of different backgrounds and traditions in the contemplation of the crucifixion.

For Additional Meditation

Mark 15

Mark's entire Gospel is shorter than the other three, and his crucifixion account is also the shortest. Read it and note the differences between it and the others.

WEDNESDAY

Reflection

Today we'll examine each of the last statements from Jesus on the cross to see what we might learn from them.

1. Jesus spoke to the Father.

In the first statement, Jesus asked the Father to forgive those who were responsible for his crucifixion, demonstrating his divine love and forgiveness. Nothing is more loving—or more difficult—than forgiveness. Jesus looked into the faces of his mocking executioners and felt only compassion for them. Anyone who followed Jesus's life and ministry should not be surprised by his desire to forgive. He taught his disciples to forgive both enemies *and* friends—seventy times seven. On the cross, he practiced what he had been preaching, forgiving his own torturers. In the midst of his excruciating suffering, the heart of Jesus focused on others rather than himself.

2. Jesus spoke to the criminal on the cross.

One of the criminals who was crucified with Christ recognized Jesus and expressed faith in him as Savior. In the Lord's response, we see God's grace poured out through faith as Jesus assured the dying man of his forgiveness and salvation. Jesus promised the man he would share eternal life with him in paradise that very day.

3. Jesus spoke to Mary and John.

When Jesus told Mary and John to view each other as mother and son, he was commanding John to care for his mother after his death. Jesus's crucifixion fulfilled the prophecy that Simeon gave to Mary when Jesus was a small child: "And a sword will pierce your own soul too" (Luke 2:35b). Jesus, knowing he would not be around to provide for his mother, as sons in that culture were expected to do, entrusted the task going forward to his faithful apostle John.

4. Jesus cried out to the Father.

In the darkest hours of his suffering, Jesus cried out the opening words of Psalm 22. Although much has been suggested regarding what Jesus may have meant by quoting this scripture at this particular moment, it seems apparent enough that Jesus was truly in agony and feeling genuinely alone. At the same time, we cannot ignore that he directly quoted Psalm 22, so we also acknowledge the fuller context of that psalm's message: in the midst of such agony, Jesus knew to whom he cried out—the Father, who alone could sustain him.

5. Jesus was thirsty.

By the time Jesus declared his thirst, it would've been difficult for him to even get a breath. Hanging by his arms, he would've had to pull himself up each time he wanted to breathe. His shoulders would've been sore and his mouth parched. He was exhausted. He asked for something to drink to wet his lips before sharing his final words. Earlier, he refused a drink of vinegar, gall, and myrrh that was offered to alleviate his suffering, fulfilling the prophecy in Psalm 69:21: "They put gall in my food and gave me vinegar for my thirst." Now, in preparation for his final statement, he acknowledged his thirst and took a few drops.

6. Jesus declared completion of his mission.

There are differing accounts of what were Jesus's actual, *final* words before dying. Both Matthew and Mark share that, just before he breathed his last, he cried out in a loud voice (see Matthew 27:50; Mark 15:37), but they do not tell us what he said. John tells us that he said, "It is finished." As we will discover in a few moments, Luke says he said something else entirely.

The three little words "It is finished" are packed with meaning. What was finished was not only Christ's earthly life, not only his suffering and dying, not only the payment for sin and the redemption of the world—but the very reason and purpose he came to earth. His final act of obedience was complete. The scriptures had been fulfilled.

The word translated "finished" is the Greek term *teleō*, which means "to complete an activity or process, bring to an end, finish, to complete something or fulfill its purpose." It is part of a word group that derives from the same root, *telos*, which has to do with goals, aims, and purposes. In John's Gospel, Jesus used a version of this word many times (*teleioō*) to indicate his intention to fulfill his purpose and bring to completion God's work in the world (see John 4:34; 5:36; 17:4).

7. Jesus spoke to the Father a final time.

When Jesus committed his spirit into the hands of the Father, he was once again quoting Scripture (Psalm 31:5). Jesus used the scriptures of the Jewish faith to demonstrate his complete trust in the heavenly Father. He entered death in the same way he lived each day of his life—offering up his life as the perfect sacrifice and placing himself in God's hands.

Jesus's final words from the cross reveal a way to respond to life's most trying moments. Instead of simply enduring death and its darkness, Jesus committed his spirit into the safe keeping of his heavenly Father. At the cross he faced life's greatest challenge, but he did not face it alone. Even when he felt alone, he was not. Though his soul felt the sting of separation, his will remained fastened with faith. When he was overwhelmed to the point of death, he chose his final words carefully, committing his spirit to the Father. We too must be willing to surrender—committing our lives, our hardships, our very souls—to the Lord.

For Additional Meditation

Psalm 22
Psalm 31

Read these two psalms that Jesus quoted from the cross. We know that Jesus knew his Hebrew Scriptures very well. Consider why phrases from these two might have come into his mind during his most painful, torturous, final moments.

_____

_____

_____

_____

_____

_____

_____

_____

_____

_____

_____

THURSDAY

Reflection

It was over. Jesus had breathed his last. The normal Roman practice was to leave the bodies of executed criminals on their crosses for weeks as part of the shame. However, Jewish law would not permit such an offense (see Deuteronomy 21:22–23); shortly after the point of death, Jewish bodies were buried in a special place. In the case of Jesus, two unlikely individuals who were both secret disciples of Jesus—Joseph of Arimathea and Nicodemus—moved quickly to ensure that Jesus would be honorably buried before the Sabbath began.

Joseph of Arimathea was an influential individual who cared deeply for Jesus. Arimathea was a town just north of Jerusalem. Mark calls Joseph a "prominent member" of the Jewish council that was called the Sanhedrin (15:43), and Luke tells us that Joseph had not approved of the Sanhedrin's decision to sentence Jesus to death (23:50–51). Joseph had apparently had enough of following Jesus in secret and, at his death, chose this moment to make his allegiance clear by going to Pilate and asking permission to take custody of Jesus's body for proper Jewish burial.

Joseph was joined in his act of mercy by Nicodemus, another member of the Sanhedrin and another secret disciple who was so afraid of his peers he was only willing to speak to Jesus under the cloak of darkness (see John 3:1–10). Later, though, he bravely and publicly questioned the Sanhedrin's prejudicial condemnation of Jesus without a hearing (7:50–52). Both Joseph and Nicodemus were wealthy men. Joseph owned a private tomb, newly hewn out of rock in a garden near Golgotha (see Matthew 27:60). It was a family tomb, but it had never been used, and Joseph made a place for the Master inside it. Nicodemus purchased expensive preparations for the burial, bringing about seventy-five pounds of myrrh and aloes.

The two of them together wrapped Jesus's body in the burial spices and linen strips "in accordance with Jewish burial customs" (John 19:40). Myrrh and aloes reduced the smell of a decaying body. Seventy-five pounds suggests a quantity that might be used at a royal burial. The compound was inserted into the linen as they wrapped each limb individually and then the body.

The Synoptic Gospels tell us that some female disciples accompanied the men bearing the body to the tomb so they would know the location when they returned after the Sabbath (see Matthew 27:61; Mark 15:47; Luke 23:55–56). Two days later, on Sunday morning, the first Easter, the women brought additional spices to complete the body's preparation, which is when they learned that he had risen!

For Additional Meditation

Isaiah 53
Philippians 2:5–11

Read these scriptures and consider what God's mission in the world through Jesus was.

_____

_____

_____

_____

_____

_____

_____

_____

_____

_____

FRIDAY

Ponder the words of this old familiar hymn, written by Charles Wesley, as you continue to think on what you've studied and learned this week.

Love Divine, All Loves Excelling (#507)

Love divine, all loves excelling, joy of heav'n, to earth come down
Fix in us thy humble dwelling; all thy faithful mercies crown
Jesus, thou art all compassion; pure, unbounded love thou art
Visit us with thy salvation; enter every trembling heart

Finish then thy new creation; pure and spotless let us be
Let us see thy great salvation, perfectly restored in thee
Changed from glory into glory, till in heav'n we take our place
Till we cast our crowns before thee, lost in wonder, love, and praise

SATURDAY IN JERUSALEM

When we returned from Jerusalem several friends asked, "What was your favorite part of the trip?" Although there were many wonderful experiences, the highlight was our first Sabbath in the Holy City. The Sabbath (or *Shabbat*) is the centerpiece of Jewish life. It is a day of rest and celebration that begins on Friday at sunset and extends until approximately an hour after nightfall on Saturday evening.

Prior to our trip, I was able to arrange for a *Shabbat* dinner with a Jewish family in their home. I worked with an organization that arranges such home visits in a variety of cities around the world. We were given the name, address, and contact information of our host. Before we went, Jill and I took some time to review the meaning and significance of the various aspects of a traditional *Shabbat* observance.

At the heart of this sacred time is the Friday evening dinner. It is a treasured ritual in Jewish tradition, encompassing elements of spirituality, family unity, gratitude, and community. It provides an opportunity for individuals to disconnect from the fast-paced world and reconnect with their loved ones and with God. Through lighting candles, reciting blessings, sharing a festive meal, and singing songs, the dinner embodies the essence of *Shabbat*, inviting participants to find peace, reflect, and recharge their spirits. In a world filled with constant busyness, the *Shabbat* dinner stands as an oasis, bearing witness to the importance of rest, connection, and the beauty of tradition.

The dinner begins with the careful preparation of the home. The atmosphere is transformed into a sanctuary, filled with warmth, tranquility, and a sense of holiness. Families take great care to set a beautiful table, typically covered with a white tablecloth and adorned with candles, flowers, and special silverware and china. The act of creating this sacred space sets the tone for the evening because it invites disconnection from the distractions of the outside world in order to embrace the spirit of *Shabbat*.

As the sun begins to set, the family gathers around the table, ready to welcome *Shabbat* with the lighting of the candles. Traditionally, two candles are lit to symbolize the dual commandments of remembering and observing *Shabbat*. The lighting signifies the transition from the ordinary week to the sanctity of *Shabbat*, filling the home with the soft glow of peace and spirituality. Following the candle lighting, the head of the household recites the *Kiddush*. This ancient blessing acknowledges the sacredness of *Shabbat* and the importance of pausing to appreciate the blessings of life. The *Kiddush* is typically recited over a cup of wine or grape juice and serves as a reminder to sanctify time and elevate the ordinary to the extraordinary.

After the *Kiddush*, two loaves of a special braided bread, called *challah*, are brought to the table. The head of the household takes the loaves, covers them with a decorative cloth, and recites what is known as the *HaMotzi* (the blessing of the bread). This blessing acknowledges God as the provider of sustenance and expresses gratitude for the bread that nourishes the body. The *challah* is then passed around, and each participant tears off a piece, symbolizing the sharing of food and fostering a sense of unity and community.

With the blessings completed, the *Shabbat* dinner follows. It is a festive meal and an opportunity for family members to connect on a more personal level than they would during the ordinary routines of busy lives. It is also a time to appreciate the abundance of God's blessings and to express gratitude for the nourishment of both body and soul. Throughout the *Shabbat* dinner, songs and prayers are recited to enhance the spiritual experience. Families often sing traditional melodies, known as *zemirot* ("table songs"), which are passed down from generation to generation. These songs evoke a sense of joy, gratitude, and unity, uplifting the spirit and deepening the connection to Jewish heritage.

During *Shabbat*, devout Jews refrain from many normal activities. For example, many do not use their phones during the Sabbath. Knowing that I would not be able to contact our host once Sabbath began, Jill and I gave ourselves plenty of time to find the place without getting lost, and we ended up arriving in the area early. Since it is just as rude to show up early as it is to come late, we located a bench outside, not far from the home, and sat down together to wait until a more appropriate time. This turned out to be a serendipitous decision. Little by little, families began to pass by on their way to their own Sabbath gatherings. As they passed, each turned to greet us with the traditional Hebrew greeting for Sabbath: *"Shabbat Shalom."* Its literal meaning is "Sabbath of peace."

When the time of our arrival approached, we walked to our host's home and were greeted warmly by a woman named Lea and her four children. Their home was lovely, and the aroma of Mideastern spices welcomed us. Our hostess had set a large, elegant table that stretched the length of the living room. As we talked, she said she was also expecting two other couples, and we were soon joined by a winsome Catholic couple from San Francisco and a Jewish father and his daughter from Cleveland. He had brought his daughter to Jerusalem for her birthday.

When it was time to begin, we all gathered at the table and stood respectfully as the hostess began the ceremony of the *Kiddush*. With a touch of drama, she set a chalice and saucer before her. Taking her time, she began to slowly pour red wine from a large pitcher into the chalice. As she did, she sang a blessing and continued to pour. We watched as the wine began to fill the cup. Once it reached the brim, we assumed she would stop pouring—but she did not! We looked on as the chalice began to overflow with wine, spilling into the saucer below. She lifted her gaze to us and said, *"We cannot contain God's blessings."* What a moment! My mind went immediately to Psalm 23.

Then came the passing of the *challah* bread. Each person broke off a portion. Everyone was reverently quiet during this part of the ceremony. Still standing, we listened as our host continued to share a series of Hebrew blessings—some spoken, others sung. Following the ceremonies of the cup and the bread, we were invited to wash our hands. This was a ceremonial washing, after which we returned to the table, took our seats, and began to converse. These rituals are repeated every week on *Shabbat*.

The meal itself was fabulous. We began with an array of salads: tomato and cucumber, spinach with pomegranate dressing, couscous, pickled slaw, and a serving of beets. Then came a huge, whole salmon with capers and lemon, followed by an array of vegetables and roasted chicken and beef. The meal concluded with our choice of Jewish apple cake and/or macaroons. At one point, Jill leaned over and whispered, "This is like having Thanksgiving in the U.S. But they do it every week!" There was much more food than we could consume, which is part of the plan. Since cooking on the Sabbath is not permitted, all the food is prepared before sundown on Friday. What is not eaten on Friday is available for lunch the following day.

During the dinner we learned something of the hostess's story and got acquainted with her children—twin fifteen-year-old daughters, a thirteen-year-old daughter, and an eleven-year-old son. The children entered the conversations with ease, telling us about their schooling, their hobbies, and their friends. In a meaningful moment during the meal, Lea called each of her children forward to embrace them individually, assuring each one of her love and offering a blessing.

After nearly two hours at the table, the meal concluded with a final blessing. We thanked our hostess and walked out into the warm breeze and a full, moonlit sky. I was reminded of an observation made by a travel writer named Mary Anne Radmacher: *I am not the same having seen the moon shine from the other side of the world.* The couple from San Francisco were staying in a hotel not far from our apartment. They told us they had walked to the dinner and invited us to walk back with them. Although it was about two miles, it was a delight to stroll through the streets and various neighborhoods of Jerusalem, discussing the different aspects of the meal and what it meant to us.

When we returned to the apartment, Jill and I sat up talking over the experience we had just shared. This dinner occurred early during our month-long stay in Jerusalem, and we both felt that if our trip had ended that day, the journey had already been worth it. We recalled together the Sabbath Sundays of our childhoods, not all that different from the Jewish observance of *Shabbat*. There was a large family meal that always began with a prayer of blessing. The activities of the day were restricted because it was a day of rest. Many stores were closed. Jill remembered that farmers in her rural area did not work in their fields, even if rain was coming—such was their respect for the Lord's Day.

Being in Jerusalem for several Sabbath days made us realize that busy is not better; that more often results in less; and that our addiction to constant activity has diminishing returns. *Shabbat* invites individuals and families into a sacred space of rest and renewal. It is a time to step away from the noise of the world, to disconnect from our screens and reconnect with our inner selves and our loved ones. As we rest, we find solace in the silence, replenishing our energy and finding peace in the moment. *Shabbat* offers us the opportunity to align our priorities with what truly matters.

EASTER SUNDAY

Scripture

Matthew 28

The angel said to the women, "Do not be afraid, for I know that you are looking for Jesus, who was crucified. He is not here; he has risen, just as he said. Come and see the place where he lay."
—*Matthew 28:5–6*

Reflection

The resurrection of Jesus falls outside the season of Lent, which ends at the close of Holy Saturday. Yet the whole focus of Lent is to prepare for the celebration. "HE IS RISEN" has echoed through the centuries in the lives of believers from every tribe and tongue. Easter Sunday is the first day of the larger season of Easter, a period of fifty days leading up to Pentecost.

From the time Jesus determined to go to Jerusalem—all the way through the events of the final Passover meal he shared with his disciples, along with the agonies of Gethsemane and the *Via Dolorosa*—Jesus remained steadfast in his determination to finish what the Father had sent him to do. His obedience and love were unfailing—all of which makes our celebration of Easter all the more meaningful.

As we consider our response to the glorious news of Easter, it is helpful to note the instructions (or imperatives) we find in Matthew 28 that represent the responses the disciples were to have to the resurrection, outlining a path forward for all of us as we leave the shadows of Lent and step into the light of Easter.

The imperatives are "come and see" (v. 6) and "go and tell" (vv. 7, 10). May the love of Christ and the empowering presence of the Holy Spirit enable each of us to "come and see" through a life-changing encounter with the resurrected Jesus; then, to embrace the mission to "go and tell." This is the Great Commission! Jesus said, "All authority in heaven and on earth has been given to me. Therefore go and make disciples of all nations, baptizing them in the name of the Father and of the Son and of the Holy Spirit, and teaching them to obey everything I have commanded you. And surely I am with you always, to the very end of the age" (vv. 18–20).

In Jerusalem

About three weeks after our *Shabbat* dinner in Jerusalem, we were walking near our apartment early on a Thursday morning when we fell into step and a friendly conversation with an older Jewish couple. He was a retired medical doctor and professor whose last name was David.

"What brings you to Jerusalem?" the gentleman asked.

"We have come just to be here for a time," I replied. "To walk the streets, meet the people, visit the holy sites, and refresh our own spirits."

In response, this couple began to give us suggestions of neighborhoods, restaurants, and places of interest known only to the locals.

"Where are you headed?" I asked.

"We are going to the market to shop for *Shabbat*," the man replied.

They began to describe their plans for the next evening and the following day. Suddenly, uncharacteristically, Jill asked, "May we come?" Once the words were said, neither of us could believe she had been bold enough to invite ourselves to the home of these strangers.

Without hesitation, the man said, "Our plans are set for tomorrow evening, but come on Saturday for our *Shabbat* lunch." He gave us the address, which happened to be in the same complex as the condo we had rented, and told us to arrive at ten minutes to twelve. "The door will be open," he added. We talked a bit longer, exchanged contact information, and agreed to see each other on Saturday.

When Saturday arrived, we walked the short distance from our front door to Dr. and Mrs. David's open door. They greeted us like family. We talked briefly and were soon joined by their son and his wife and young children. After their arrival, everyone was invited to the table, where Dr. David began the meal with a series of Hebrew blessings followed by his taking a large loaf of *challah*, salting it generously, tearing off portions, and tossing the pieces to each of us. "You are never to ask for bread," he said. "We are not beggars. We receive the bread as children of our heavenly Father."

They served a delicious meal of cold dishes as we talked about the blessings of *Shabbat*, their family history, and the relationship between Israel and the United States. After the meal, the table was cleared, and Jill was invited into the kitchen. Jewish regulations restrict the kinds of work that may and may not be done on *Shabbat*. One can clear the table and wash the dishes by hand but cannot use any electronic devices like radios, televisions, computers, cell phones, or kitchen appliances. It is permissible, in keeping with Jewish regulations, to load a dishwasher, but since it is an electric appliance, no one from an orthodox family can actually push the start button. On this occasion, Mrs. David seemed very pleased to have a non-Jewish guest who would be permitted to start the dishwasher. Jill was happy to oblige.

As we walked back to our place, we gave thanks for the gift of another sacred *Shabbat* and the hospitality of strangers, who by the end of the meal had become friends. Sabbath is not simply the pause that refreshes. It is the pause that transforms.

After sundown on Saturday, life resumes its normal pace in Jerusalem. The greeting *Shabbat Shalom* is replaced with *Shavua Tov. Shavua* is the Hebrew word for "week," and *Tov* is the Hebrew word for "good." So, having been replenished spiritually and physically by a *Shabbat Shalom*—a peaceful *Shabbat*, a day of rest—Jews wish each other a good week: *Shavua Tov!*

My cup runneth over.